ASSOCIATED FACULTY PRESS, INC.

POLICY STUDIES ORGANIZATION SERIES PUBLICATIONS

McCall and Weber — Social Science and Public Policy
Rosenbloom — Public Personnel Policy: The Politics of Civil Service
Hadden — Risk Analysis Institutions, and Public Policy
Redburn, Buss, and Ledebur — Revitalizing The American Economy

350
R595

Manufactured in the United States of America

Published by
Associated Faculty Press, Inc.
Port Washington, New York

Library of Congress Cataloging in Publication Data
Main entry under title:

Risk Analysis, Institutions, and Public Policy

  (A Policy Studies Organization series publication)
  Includes bibliographical references and index.
  1. Risk management—Addresses, essays, lectures.
2. Risk—Government policy—United States—Addresses,
essays, lectures. I. Hadden, Susan G. II. Series.
HD61.R56 1984   350   83-15792
ISBN 0-8046-9332-3

85-3199

TABLE OF CONTENTS

LIST OF ILLUSTRATIONS

LIST OF TABLES

ACKNOWLEDGMENTS

As anyone who has edited a book knows, the major thanks must go to the authors of the chapters. In general, they have been extremely cooperative in meeting deadlines and in complying with endless requests to shorten; all were also very patient in awaiting news about both versions of this symposium.

I am also indebted to the Lyndon B. Johnson Foundation, a grant from which funded the earlier version of the symposium and made publication in book form possible. The Policy Studies Organization also contributed time and effort.

ABOUT THE CONTRIBUTORS

John B. Graham was a research associate at the Brookings Institution, Washington, D.C. In 1983-84 he is serving on the faculty at the Harvard School of Public Health.

Susan G. Hadden is an associate professor at the Lyndon B. Johnson School of Public Affairs at the University of Texas at Austin.

Michael B. Kraft is professor of political science and public administration at the University of Wisconsin at Green Bay.

Steve Rayner is a senior research associate at the Centre for Occupational and Community Research, Middlesex Politechnic. Since completing this article, the author has assumed a research appointment at the Oak Ridge National Laboratory.

Walter Rosenbaum is professor of political science at the University of Florida at Gainesville.

Mark Rushefsky is assistant professor of political science at the University of Florida.

Norman J. Vig is professor of political science and director of the Science Technology and Public Policy program at Carleton College.

W. Kip Viscusi is director of the Center for the Study of Business Regulation, an IBM research professor, FUQUA School of Business, Duke University.

William C. Wood is assistant professor of economics at the University of Virginia.

PART I
RISK ANALYSIS, INSTITUTIONS, AND PUBLIC POLICY

Chapter 1

INTRODUCTION:
RISK POLICY IN AMERICAN INSTITUTIONS
Susan G. Hadden

Risks, especially risks to health, safety, and the environment, are receiving increasing attention from policymakers and the public. Often, risk legislation has been enacted in response to dramatic disasters which have gained public attention. The result is a multiplicity of policies toward risk, with similar risks treated differently and responsibility for one kind of risk lodged in several different agencies. Thus, existing structures for controlling risk are complex and fragmented. Moreover, the current state of policies toward risk is one of flux, with regulations and legislation in many areas about to be promulgated or changed. Many decisions await new technical information on the nature of particular risks or on ways to control known risks.

While there is considerable awareness of these gaps in the technical underpinnings of risk policies, both scholars and policymakers have tended to slight the need for understanding of the institutional factors in controlling risk. The purpose of this volume is to provide a more systematic approach to understanding the role institutions play in the formation and implementation of policies designed to reduce risks to health, safety, or the environment. [1]

Taken together, the essays in this volume constitute an argument for adopting a new model of the process of risk regulation—a model that consists of multiple stages in which both technical and political considerations are taken into account. By adopting this model, the authors are, whether explicitly or implicitly, criticizing another widely-used model, which I shall call the ''two-stage'' model.

3

In a seminal work in the area of risk policy, Lowrance (1976) divided risk assessment into two stages: measurement of the risk and determination of its acceptability. The first stage is conducted by scientists; the second by politicians. Because the two stages are temporally distinct, with the political determination of risk acceptability following its technical identification and measurement, I believe that the model implies an inferior status for the second stage. The science drives the political assessment.

I have termed this model the two-stage model, rather than the Lowrencian model, in part because some of his later writings suggest that the originator recognizes that the model may be too simplified (see, for example, Lowrance 1980). Many other writers have adopted the model, however. (Rushefsky's paper in this volume notes some of them.) Believing that the first was the more important stage, they have concentrated on perfecting the technical analysis. The fact that many of these writers have been scientists, engineers, or economists has encouraged their adoption of a model that reinforces their natural bias towards technical rather than political bases for decision-making.

The papers in this book suggest a variety of reasons why the two-stage model is inadequate:

1. The temporal distinction between the stages is difficult to maintain. As we shall see below, Congress writes laws that provide guidelines within which agencies must control risks. This means that both the legislative and the executive branches are making technical and political risk assessments; often each makes more than one. Kraft surveyed both members of Congressional staffs and agency personnel; he documents the ways in which they undertake to make both kind of judgments. Vig's paper on the courts introduces the complications caused by the third branch becoming involved in risk policy; some decisions reflect scientific as well as procedural bases for judicial involvement.

2. It is difficult to separate so completely the technical from other values. Rayner argues that cultural values—he distinguishes entrepreneurial, hierarchical, and egalitarian group value systems—override all other bases for assessing risks. Rushefsky's paper for the earlier version of this symposium (1982) made quite explicit the ways in which values affect scientists' interpretation of data; he used that conclusion in his paper in this volume to suggest some inadequacies in an arrangement that calls for ''settling'' the scientific questions before turning to other parts of the decision-making process. (Also see Nemetz and Vining 1981.)

3. Changes in scientific information trigger new cycles of policymaking. The same is true for economic and even political factors. Viscusi's study of White House review of proposed agency risk regulations makes very clear that new information causes a reassessment of proposed policies; Vig's study of the courts makes the

same point although the information is not new, only subjected to a somewhat different interpretation. Wood presents a case in which new information was not assimilated into policy, and shows the dangers policymakers face by being so insensitive. Rosenbaum shows that failure to include explicitly institutional goals in initial policy formulations results in later crises that require new policy responses.

4. Finally, the two-stage model ignores the complexities of a federal system composed of diverse interests. Technical analyses differ depending on which interest makes them; assessment of risk acceptability diverge still more widely. Graham's study of restraints designed to reduce the injuries from automobile crashes shows the importance of a wide variety of actors, ranging in that instance from automobile salesmen to a federal regulatory agency. Not only are several levels of government involved in such decisions, but successful control of the risk depends on the risk assessments made by millions of individual drivers.

The model I propose is a more complicated one; it is not fully elaborated and is intended to be suggestive rather than definitive. It is shown in Figure 1, which also illustrates the two-stage model. My model is intended to illustrate the assumption that while the policy decision depends on the scientific (and explicitly on the economic) risk assessments, it constitutes not an inferior but rather the most important part of the process. Thus, it is placed at the top of the triangle that represents the process. At the same time, because political and institutional concerns also inform the underlying technical analyses, each element is connected to the others. Finally, the process is iterative; as the component elements change, the process is renewed and incremental changes are made. However, it would not be efficient for the entire process to begin again, and procedures must be designed that allow for refinements of policy without full-dress review; thus the ensuing triangles. are both smaller in diameter and to the right (subsequent) to those representing the initial stage. While the proposed model could profit from further refinement, it marks an important break with past writings in the field. We hope that it supplants the two-stage model, so that future writers will have a firmer basis for considering the complex process that constitutes the making of risk policy.

WHY RISK POLICY IS DIFFERENT

The model proposed here is not very different from others already formulated for other parts of the policy process. Why does risk policy deserve special treatment? The reasons derive from one special feature of risk analysis: the predominance of its scientific and technical component.

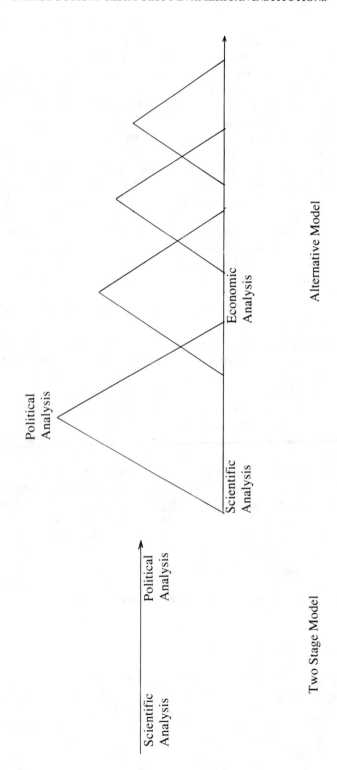

Figure 1. Two Models of the Risk Policy Process

The very definition of risk highlights this characteristic. Although risk has been defined in a variety of ways, for our purposes an ordinary-language definiton will suffice. "Risk" expresses some likelihood that something harmful or undesirable will occur, and sois a joint consideration of probability and of (adverse) consequences. [2] Consequences are in turn composed of two factors: how many people are affected (magnitude); and the exact nature of the consequences to those affected (severity). This definition highlights what must be done to control a risk: reduce its magnitude or severity or both. [3] Yet in order to implement a policy that successfully accomplishes either of these goals, we must be able to understand the path by which the risk accrues, which in turn requires that we obtain technical information about it. Determining which risks to control first—which are most "risky"—entails knowing and comparing probabilities and consequences, which are again often learned through technical analysis.

Another reason that risk is so closely related to scientific information is that many risks arise as unanticipated side effects of using new technologies. Although each technology brings many benefits, each also carries risks, many of which are unanticipated and many of which do not become manifest for decades. Because they are unexpected and difficult to identify, these risks are often, like economic externalities, imposed on people who do not benefit proportionately from the attendant technology. Policies to control risks therefore have two characteristics—uncertainty of information, and redistributive consequences—that make policymakers reluctant to become involved in risk policies. This means that institutional arrangements to control risk are unusually fragmented and complex as each authority attempts to pass responsibility on to another.

Measuring (?) Risk

In the two-stage model, political choices follow technical assessments of risk. One reason that the model is not entirely applicable is that the technical assessments are often difficult to make or unclear in their policy implications. The uncertainties of technical information not only allow policymakers often to site selectively that portion of the scientific evidence that supports decisions made on other bases, but also create demands for elaborate procedures to ensure multiple reviews of all information. It is worth reviewing briefly why some of these uncertainties arise; most of these points are elaborated in the other papers.

First, probabilities of risks to health, safety, and the environment are often difficult to measure. While the probabilities in games of chance are subject to a priori or logical determination, the likelihood that health or the environment will be adversely affected by a particular act is not. In fact, ascertaining the probability distributions of a risk with any degree of confidence requires frequent experience with the adverse consequences, and even then our "measurement" of the probability remains an educated guess. Although we may attempt to simulate these risks through laboratory tests on animals or with computer models, or conduct epidemiological studies to determine the circumstances under which there will be direct effects on human health, many uncertainties will always remain.

Psychological studies also indicate that people often have difficulty assessing probabilities accurately even in those cases when they are more measurable. For example, people tend to believe that risks that are controllable, understood, or have immediate consequences are "less risky" than otherwise similar risks that are not controllable, not understood, or that have delayed consequences. The more certain that death will result from exposure to an agent, the more risky it is perceived to be, even when the probability of the fatal event is extremely low. (Kahneman, Slovic, and Tversky 1982; Fischhoff 1977; Starr 1969). Graham (1982) suggests other kinds of biases that affect perceptions of both individuals and agencies, including dislike of allowing risks to accrue to identifiable individuals, such as those working in a particular industry.

A good example of the kinds of misperceptions just summarized is provided by a long-time resident of a Missouri town where large concentrations of a highly toxic chemical were found in the dirt:

> I imagine I've probably eaten, inhaled, and had on my body in open cuts more mud than anone else [in town]. I roll in the mud when I work and I'm in as good health as anybody. They'll have to prove it before I'll believe it. [4]

When people assess probabilities incorrectly, they prefer policy responses that are inappropriate. While many critics of current government policies believe that people tend to demand too much governmental interference (Wildavsky 1979), there are many instances of the opposite case, as when people demand the removal of laws requiring motorcyclists to wear helmets.

Severity is equally difficult to measure. One common measure of toxicity, for example, is the LD50, or the amount of a substance that is lethal to half the test animals within a specified time. Using a common metric, milligrams per kilogram of body weight, it is relatively easy to compare LD50's for various substances—in the laboratory animals. Extrapolation to humans, however, is not straightforward; one substance may affect humans in the same way as it affects cats but not dogs, another may do the opposite. Even with such difficulties, the relative immediacy of the effect makes toxicity much easier to measure than effects that do not occur for many years; among the confounding effects are different individual sensitivities to exposure, possible interactive effects among substances, and, foremost, the absence of a model that shows how the causal agent produces the unwanted effect. [5] In addition, assessment of severity is also subject to perceptual biases: some people skydive, while others are reluctant to go outside at night.

The difficulties of measuring risks are exacerbated when it is necessary to compare them, since this entails trading off among the incommensurate dimensions of risks: probability, severity, and magnitude. Their different responses to automotiles and to accidents in nuclear power plants suggest that many people are willing to accept a high probability, low consequencerisk over a low probability, high consequence risk. However, the case is less clear-cut when the risk is of high probability among a very limited group, as in the case of many occupational hazards, or of moderate probability and severity.

These difficulties in measuring risks confound policymaking. It is hard to devise acceptable policies when people do not even agree that there is a need for a social response; the difficulty is exacerbated when the paths by which the risks occur are poorly understood and policies will be of uncertain effectiveness. Attempts to resolve some of the scientific uncertainties in assessing risk—attempts such as the science panels discussed by Rushefsky in this volume—have only highlighted the basis of technical assessments in other kinds of values.

CURRENT INSTITUTIONAL RESPONSES TO RISK

The model of risk policy proposed here is not explicit about the institutional locus of the different risk assessments. In fact, as the papers by Kraft and others show, identification of a risk may come from any one of several sources, and elaboration of a policy response may also occur in any of the three branches of government. Because each policy response must ultimately be based in law, however, I begin with a brief examination of three characteristics of Congressional response to risk.

The first feature of Congressional response is the use of a variety of risk standards. Although some of the differences in risk standards reflect changes in Congressional attitude to risk over time, there is no neat evolutionary pattern to be distinguished. Field (1981) distinguishes three kinds of risk standards: risk-only; technology-only; and balancing. The first is strictest in some sense, since it allows the implementing agency to consider only the health effects of the substance to be regulated, while technology-only laws call for regulations to be based on the existing capabilities of technology to reduce risk. Finally, balancing laws, of which most recent risk laws are examples, explicitly call for agencies to identify tradeoffs between health or environmental values and social or economic costs.

A second feature of Congressional risk control is the number of committees to which oversight of each risk law is entrusted. This fragmentation of Congressional authority is partly a reflection of fragmentation of agency authority, which in turn is a result of Congress' former tendency to promulgate very narrow risk laws and to place enforcement power for related statutes in different agencies. For example, administration and enforcement of the Flammable Fabrics Act Amendments of 1967 was delegated to no less than four agencies—the departments of Commerce, Health, Education, and Welfare (HEW), Treasury, and the Federal Trade Commission. Oversight responsibility by a multiplicity of committees also exhibits a typical response to program complexity—a commensurate increase in complexity of the controlling organization, and especially an increase in the redundancy of controls (Anthony 1982). When so many units have responsibility, none can bear too much of the blame for failure.

Finally, an examination of risk laws such as those discussed in the papers in this volume suggests that Congress has largely avoided a role as a determiner of acceptable risk. We have noted the reasons for this above: risk policies create a lot of political pressure because of their salience and redistributive implications, so legislators prefer to avoid making decisions that will necessarily be opposed by some constituents. Furthermore, the need to respond to changes and uncertainties of technical information makes it an area that is inappropriate for detailed Congressional oversight; rather, it meets the usual criteria for delegation to regulatory authorities. What others (Lilley and Miller 1977) have called the "new social regulation," resulting in the establishment of many new regulatory agencies, is perhaps better understood as an extension of the usual Congressional response to highly technical policies.

Agencies

While the laws enacted by Congress provide the major determinant of the ways in which agencies decide to control risks, other political and internal agency factors are also important. For example, Mendeloff (1979) shows that the Occupational Safety and Health Administration (OSHA) is very responsive to labor unions' requests for stringent safety and risk standards. Graham (1981) discusses the special factors that acount for the ways in which agencies act, and especially the differences in apparent risk standards used by agencies. Among these factors are public demand for reducing risks to victims who are identifiable ex ante, or who are identifiable ex post when causality is clear, the degree to which collective actions appears to be necessary to control a risk, the visibility of the costs to control the risk, and the level of uncertainty surrounding the risk itself.

Both the looseness of most statutory language and the variety of the risks they are to control give agencies considerable leeway in the regulatory approaches they choose. Agencies probably have more flexibility under the balancing than under the other kinds of mandates, although it should be noted that the multiplicity of risk statutes itself gives agencies considerable leeway. For example, the Food and Drug Administration (FDA) has managed to avoid using the Delaney Clause (a "risk-only" standard) and looked instead to other mandates when it wishes to permit certain food additives to be used.

The definition of risk as the probability of adverse consequences suggested that risk control policies must either reduce severity or magnitude of risks, or move to a different probability state. Agency activities can be categorized in that way:

- determine that risk is acceptable and take no action.
- change the probability state and reduce the likelihood that the unwanted event will occur: ban the causal agent, reduce the frequency of use of the causal agent, build in safeguards, give directions for safe use.
- reduce the severity of consequences: ban the causal agent, reduce the intensity of use of the causal agent, build in safeguards, give directions for safe use.
- reduce the number of people affected: ban the causal agent, reduce the frequency, intensity, and geographical area in which the agency is used; create standards based on the most sensitive; give directions (and training) for safe use.

Classifying by the nature of the regulatory action rather than by its goal, we obtain the following list, loosely in order of regulatory rigor:

1. Do nothing; let the market control the risk.
2. Perfect the market by providing information or requiring its provision: label products, provide test data to regulatory agency, manifest system for tracking hazardous wastes, consumer education.
3. Perfect the market by forcing production units to internalize all costs: pollution taxes, creating markets in pollution rights.
4. Employ nonmarket solutions: ban substances, set emissions standards.

Agencies have thus far tended to rely on the nonmarket solutions, although provision of information through labeling is also widely used, often because it is specified by law. Labeling is attractive because it implicitly delegates the risk decision to each individual, thereby avoiding problems associated with aggregating individual risk preferences and with comparing risks. Labeling and other kinds of information provision requirements are enforced by at least eight agencies.

Perhaps the most widely-used technique for regulation of risk is development of standards. There are two major kinds of standards that can be used. Performance standards are usually quantitative standards that specify a goal to be met. Examples are concentrations of pollutants that may be emitted into the air, or the amount of pressure a boiler wall should withstand. Process standards specify how the regulated party is to act; the implication is that the goal is met if the process is correctly applied.

Examples are specifying the kinds of scrubber a factory must have on its stacks, or the thickness of the boiler wall. Performance standards are explicitly related to a risk control goal, while process standards are related only implicitly. Performance standards encourage innovation to meet the goal, while process standards discourage innovation, even if a more stringent goal could be met using an alternative method. However, process standards are often easier to enforce than performance standards, attainment of which must be carefully and frequently measured at "the end of the pipe," outside the production system. Because of the relative ease of enforcement, because process standards embody an existing technology rather than forcing innovation, and because process standards are frequently devised in consultation with the regulated industry, they are becoming increasingly common. The process specified by the standard often becomes the goal of the policy, replacing the less achievable and politically more distant goal of reducing risk.

In fact, process standards are only one illustration of a tendency on the part of agencies to respond to uncertainties about risk by elaborating on proedural requirements. Again, blame is dispersed along with authority. Among the kinds of procedures that have been injected into the implementation of risk laws are: specification of protocols for laboratory tests on animals; elaboration of procedures for review of proposed regulations by affected groups; establishment of committees of outside experts; and requirements for risk-benefit analyses. Many of these procedures have been devised in response to criticisms by the courts, discussed below by Vig. Agencies also found that a detailing of procedure provided a veneer of technical respectability to an inherently political activity.

Banning, another nonmarket technique of risk control, has been employed rather infrequently, although the threat remains a potent one. Rather than ban products, agencies have placed various restrictions on their uses or on users (as in medicine available by prescription only). For example, the Environmental Protection Agency (EPA) often reduces the kinds of pests or the kinds of crops for which a pesticide is approved; the Rebutable Presumption Against Registration (RPAR) process which EPA uses to review pesticides that appear to be especially risky to the environment or to man has resulted in voluntary withdrawal of several pesticides and in limitations on use, but in no outright bans. (The RPAR process illustrates our more general point as well: stages 2 and 3 of the process, originally defined respectively as a technical assessment and a risk-benefit assessment, have now been merged in practice.) Similarly, the Consumer Product Safety Commission has banned completely only a handful of products since its inception, among them a water proofing paint that exploded in the presence of a lighted match, carbon tetrachloride for home use, and paints containing more than a very small proportion of lead.

The large role that scientific information plays in risk regulation has perhaps affected the agencies more than any other part of government.

They have developed a variety of responses, virtually all of which entail several reviews of the technical bases for decision-making. Even within the agencies, therefore, risk analysis is a multi-stage process.

Courts

For over a hundred years, British and American courts have served as arbiters in cases concerning risks of products to individual consumers. Throughout most of that period, the related doctrines of "limited liability" or "negligence" prevailed. Briefly, these doctrines required that an injured party show both, (1) that the producer know that his product was defective or otherwise likely to cause an injury, and (2) that the injury he sustained was directly related to the alleged defect. These burdensome requirements did indeed place severe limits on the responsibility of the manufacturer. During the decade or so from the mid-1950s onward, however, these doctrines rapidly fell into disrepute and were replaced by the doctrine of "strict liability." It imposes much more of a burden on manufacturers, who are responsible for injuries sustained from "foreseeable" uses of their product's known risks. Product liability thus rapidly became a field in which the court was required to make technical assessments of each product's risk, balancing costs of different kinds of remedies against the probability and severity of the risk itself.

The increased burden thus placed on the court has its parallel in the litigation arising from federal risk standards of all kinds. Although the court has always been able to review regulations to safeguard against agency abuse, the increased use of scientific evidence as a basis for rules opened the door for a new court role. Vig's paper in this volume shows that while some courts did feel free to review and decide upon scientific evidence, the courts have now reverted to their former emphasis on procedure. In response to court pressure, however, agencies have become much more careful about their collection and interpretation of scientific evidence.

The court's retreat from substantive review of risk evidence was probably appropriate. Many observers question the ability of the courts to arbitrate technical questions. The decision rendered by the Supreme Court in the "benzene case" (*Industrial Union Department* v. *API*; 448 US 607, 1980), in which no two Justices used the same reasoning to reach a conclusion, suggests that an active role in reviewing the validity of technical data poses threats to the court's own institutional legitimacy. Rushefsky's article in this volume notes a related objection to substantive review: the incompatibility of the adversarial judicial system with the search of science for accuracy. It is often argued that government should reduce the amount of risk regulation and allow individuals who are seriously injured to obtain damages through the court. Such arguments ignore both the distributive implications of such a plan—few people have the resources to face large companies in court—and the serious burdens this would place on the institution of the courts.

RISK-BENEFIT ANALYSIS AND INSTITUTIONS

The complexity of the issues underlying choices of risk control strategies has led to an elaboration of procedural requirements. These requirements include not only administrative procedures, including avenues of appeal and periods for notice and comment, but also scientific procedures, such as methods for conducting laboratory experiments. Specification of the composition of technical advisory committees span both the administrative and the scientific. One of the most widely-employed procedural requirements calls for agencies to perform risk-benefit analysis.

Reliance on this method springs from several sources, including the courts and the White House. Viscusi's article below discusses the White House regulatory review process; Kraft and Rosenbaum also consider it. Risk-benefit analysis is a variation of cost-benefit analysis that attempts to account for the safety as well as the economic aspects of decisions. Both methodologies are strongly dependent on the ability to assign values to items that may not lend themselves readily to quantification. We have already discussed the difficulties of "measuring" the probability and consequences of risks. This leads to a tendency to undervalue benefits since so many are intangible and especially difficult to quantify, and a tendency to overvalue costs. A recent study by EPA found that industry, from which many estimates of costs of regulation are of necessity obtained, tended to overestimate those costs significantly (US EPA 1980).

One of the most controversial aspects of risk-benefit analysis lies in the value assigned to life. By choosing a sufficiently high value, any regulation can be made to have a benefit-cost ratio higher than one (that is, have benefits exceed costs). Values of life, now used implicitly by agencies, vary by several orders of magnitude; studies of current regulatory measures show imputed values of life up to several hundred million dollars (Graham 1982). A variety of methods are available for determining values of life, including discounted future earnings, which results in lower values for lives of the elderly, blue-collar workers, and women; this method is also used in most personal injury cases and makes it difficult for residents of retirement homes even to engage an attorney to press a suit. Another method of computing the value of life computes future consumption. Zeckhauser and Shepard (1976) have defined the concept of QALY, or qualify adjusted life year, to take into account the difference between, for example, an invalid and a healthy person. While there are clear differences between qualities of different lives, evaluation of these ex ante for policy decisions seems to be beyond our present capacities (Linnerooth 1975).

Increased use of risk-benefit analysis in government despite these difficulties of measurement reflects an important development. It is part of the movement towards the "scientific state" (Schmandt 1981). Use of an apparently objective and scientific analytic technique both renders the ensuing policy decision more acceptable and fulfills expectations of professionalism by observers inside and outside government. However, reliance on technical justifications for policy poses a risk too: manipulation of risk-benefit analysis to justify political decisions may undermine peoples' beliefs in the objectivity of all kinds of technical analysis. The discounting of these tools will expose all institutions to even more severe political pressures. The risk, I am suggesting, lies not in political decisions but in the attempts of policymakers both to use science as evidence when it suits their needs, and to use its inadequacies as a justification for ignoring it when the evidence points in the "wrong" direction. This difficulty can be circumvented by avoiding the trap of believing that when scientific information exists, it must form the basis for policymaking, and by acknowledging the validity of institutions that are political in nature.

NEW INSTITUTIONAL ARRANGEMENTS

Given the complexity of the organizational arrangements that have arisen to control risk and the difficulties of determining whether and how risks should be regulated, it is not surprising that there have been many demands and suggestions for new institutions to manage risk.

One attractive kind of proposal eliminates the need for complex social risk-benefit calculi and for expenditure of social resources on regulatory decision-making and enforcement by relying more heavily on the market. Howard (1980) suggests a market for risky products in which manufacturers rate their products according to how much insurance for damages the consumer is purchasing with them. For example, lawn mowers might be available that are rated at $5,000, $10,000, and $25,000. If the user were seriously injured in using the lawn mower, he would receive the rated amount for damages; presumably, the $25,000 mower would actually be safer, although it is possible that its higher price might reflect only the higher cost of its implicit insurance.

A more frequent proposal calls for more coordination and perhaps centralization of risk policymaking. The presidential initiatives cited above derived as much from desires to control and coordinateas from desires to be economically efficient. In August, 1977, four agencies with special responsibilities for risk control—the Consumer Product Safety Commission, the Environmental Protection Agency, the Food and Drug Administration, and the Occupational Safety and Health Administration—formed the Interagency Regulatory Liaison Group (IRLG) to share information and avoid duplication of regulatory effort. Joined later by other agencies, the group attempted to establish a generic carcinogen policy. Unfortunately, this centralization effort suffered from problems common to many similar attempts (Zimmerman 1982): agency heads were not required to relinquish any authority to the centralized group; agency staff assigned to the IRLG were from the wrong departments, insufficiently informed about agency policy, and not from the correct scientific disciplines; and, finally, no one really had the responsibility for coordinating among the agencies, so agreements were hard to reach and virtually impossible to implement (Grumbly 1982). Both the IRLG and the Regulatory Council, established by President Carter in 1978, were dissolved by President Reagan. Another means for responding to the need for responding to risks rather than to laws has been internal agency reorganization. As yet, this response is poorly documented. Schmandt (1982) gives a clear example of its occurrence inside EPA, where the development of an "integrated toxics strategy" has been attempted.

Other commentators have been less concerned with institutional forms than with decision strategies. Arbitration, mediation, and negotiation, means of resolving risk issues that reduce confrontation, impose their own institutional requirements, however. Most must be conducted on a rather small scale, rendering them generally unsuited to formulation of national policy. Their compatibility with efficient use of complex technical information has yet to be explored fully as well (Amy 1982; Hadden 1981). Rushefsky's article in this volume considers the role of mediation in more detail. Like the other process requirements that we have discussed above, mediation and related techniques may influence policy or they may be used to defuse opposition.

It is interesting that so few of the proposals for new institutions represent radical reforms. This may be a reflection of the realization than the stresses imposed on existing institutions by risk policy are unlikely to be easily weathered by new institutions. It may also reflect an underlying realization that, difficult though they are, the problems presented by risk policy are not so different from those presented by many other kinds of policy, problems that our existing institutions have been designed to resolve.

It seems to me that many of the calls for new institutions can be traced to the dissatisfaction that is inevitable when we rely on the two-stage risk assessment model. To satisfy the requirements of that model institutions must be so designed as to provide for a scientific assessment of risk and to use that as the primary basis for decision-making, superimposing political values when necessary but relying on the scientific determination when it is available. The alternative model, however, conforms more to reality and suggests the possibility of modifying existing institutions.

The differences between the two models can perhaps be illustrated by reference to a question that arises about the proper place of risk perception in policymaking. We indicated above that individuals' assessments of risk are subject to a variety of perceptual biases, biases that make them overestimate the likelihoods of risks they have recently heard about, and underestimate the likelihoods of risks with which they are very familiar, such as driving automobiles. The question, which has been posed by no less a body than the National Research Council, is whether these biased risk perceptions should form the basis for public policy. The technocratic answer is that they should not, since they will cause resources to be mis-allocated towards reducing a less serious risk and away from reducing a more serious risk. (This position is clearly articulated by Paul Slovic in U.S. Congress Joint Hearings, 1980, 187−88.) The two-stage model would adopt this view, since the decision is to be made on the basis of what is *known* about the risk, including its probability. The model proposed here provides a much less definitive answer, allowing for the possibility that perceptions can influence policy because costs of allocating resources to controlling the ''wrong'' risk may well be offset by the benefits of providing so many citizens with peace of mind.

A contradiction inherent in the ''scientific state'' is that respect for science elevates its utility as a basis for policy at the same time that the inability of science to meet all the demands placed upon it by policymakers must undermine its credibility. The two-stage model of risk assessment makes this contradiction inevitable. The proposed model, however, removes some of the pressures to resolve conflicts from the scientific part of the process and places them in their rightful, political sphere. Thus the model is at the same time less ''technocentric'' than the earlier one and less likely to undermine the credibility of scientific information as a basis for policy. It also specifically acknowledges the need for continuing responsiveness to changes in both the technical and political contexts.

The most important point to emerge from the papers presented in this volume is that institutional goals and political considerations are legitimate in a political process, which the process surrounding decisions to control risks will continue to be. Domination of the risk analysis field by economists, psychologists, and toxicologists has caused this simple truism to be lost in a forest of strategies for measuring risks and treating them efficiently. Issues that are redistributive, that are based on technical information that is characterized by uncertainty, and that affect individuals' own health and quality of life are issues that must forever be political. Refinements of political institutions should therefore be designed to improve participation of affected parties and to elicit relevant information— in other words, to perfect the process by which all public decisions are made, not just those associated with controlling risks to health, safety, and the environment. While risk policy will continue to constitute an important challenge to democratic institutions, it also demonstrates their continuing strength. This volume should be but the beginning of an exploration of this neglected aspect of risk policy.

NOTES

1.   An earlier version of this symposium was published in the *Policy Studies Review* 1 (May, 1982). Insofar as the papers here overlap with those in that symposium, they have been completely revised and expanded. One point of the revisions was to highlight the institutional issues that are the focus of this work, since the earlier symposium constituted a more general introduction to risk policy.

2.   Frank Knight (1921) made a famous distinction between "risk," in which the probability of harm is known or at least knowable, and "uncertainty," in which the probability cannot be known. This definition is still widely used by economists. However, it does not coincide with the ordinary language definition, which is the more important usage in considering public policy. For a definition of risk similar to the one employed here, see Lowrance (1980).

3.   A program implemented by human beings cannot directly change the probability of a particular risk, but it can change the conditions so that everyone is in a different, more desirable state in which probabilities are lower. For example, under current conditions, the probability of being killed in an auto accident is 1 in a million for each 140 miles driven. (Wilson, 1979, 40.) We cannot change that probability, *given current conditions*, but we could move to a different probability state by prohibiting drivers who are drunk or by requiring air bags.

4.   Quoted in Bill Rose, "Dioxin stalkers walk in valley of death," *Austin American-Statesman*, Jaunary 16, 1983.

5.   There is an extensive literature on the problems of determining long-term health effects. One important assessment is found in OSHA's proposal for instituting generic regulations concerning carcinogens; see 41 FR 54, 156–161 (1977). For a shorter review, see Weisberger and Williams (1981).

PART II
CURRENT RISK CONTROL STRATEGIES

Chapter 2

RISK ANALYSIS IN REGULATORY DECISION-MAKING:

PERSPECTIVES FROM THE AGENCIES AND CAPITOL HILL
Michael E. Kraft

Editor's Introduction

The papers in this secton consider aspects of the present institutional arrangements for managing risk. Rather than providing a comprehensive picture of the relationships between institutions and risk management, the three studies focus on especially important questions raised by the present process.

Kraft's paper provides us with insight into the risk policymaking process in Congress and the agencies by focusing on the ways in which the two branches make use of risk-benefit analysis. The technique, which is an extension of cost-benefit analysis, has increasingly served as the means for combining the scientific and economic analyses of proposed regulations. In that sense, its use supports the two-stage model by combining all technical analyses into one stage, and leaving political analysis for another. On the other hand, the very fact that there have been separate scientific and economic analyses suggests a different model. Indeed, Kraft explicitly notes the development within agencies of a three-stage model. His conversations with agency staff make quite clear, however, that the "stages" are not distinct temporally, though they may involve different personnel.

The analyses that precede the passage of risk control laws by Congress are characterized by a confounding of the technical and political stages to an even greater extent than those of the agencies. Only a few Congressmen and a slightly larger proportion of staff have been involved enough in risk-benefit analysis to know that they could delegate resolution of technical difficulties to other actors without relinquishing a more general level of control over details. However, for Congress to assume confidently a more general role in risk oversight, it must gain an increased level of understanding of risk-benefit analysis—an understanding that is ironically impeded by the present emphasis by practitioners on resolution of technical and methodological issues.

Policymakers, administrators, and scholars familiar with risk analysis argue that it is an increasingly important tool in federal health, safety and environmental regulation. Governments, they say, cannot create a risk-free environment and marginal improvements in risk reduction may be costly. Thus, there is a need for sound methods of measuring risks and procedures for determining acceptable levels of risks to human health and environmental quality. However, the precise role that methods of risk analysis can or should play in regulatory decision-making is a matter of some disagreement, and has only recently become a focus of systematic study. (Rowe 1977; Lave 1983; Baram 1982; Swartzman, Liroff, and Croke 1982).

The term risk analysis is used here to refer to the combination of two activities: risk assessment and risk evaluation. Risk assessment includes the identification of risks and the estimation of the probability and severity of harm associated with them. Risk evaluation refers to the process of determining the acceptability of risks. In this usage, which is consistent with Lowrance (1976), risk assessment may be considered to be chiefly a technical activity while risk evaluation is a political determination which is necessarily based on some explicit or implicit criteria of the social acceptability of risk.

As Hadden notes in the introductory essay, the separation of risk assessment and risk evaluation is, in practice, quite difficult. In effect, agencies charged with regulation of technological risks must perform the technical assessments *and* make some judgments about the acceptability of risk.   In enacting the statutes governing those decisions, Congress has delegated broad authority for defining the level of risk considered to be in the public interest. But insofar as statutes set the boundaries within which agencies must make those evaluative judgments, risk evaluation in the legislative process precedes the technical task of risk assessment. The merger of these two activities in regulatory decision-making, and the temporal sequence noted, are insufficiently acknowledged in most writing about technological risk analysis. This chapter attempts to clarify these distinctions by examining both agency and legislative perspectives on the value and use of risk analysis. The first half of the chapter focuses on the more technical and administrative processes of risk assessment in regulatory agencies. The second half reviews some evidence on congressional involvement with risk analysis, especially its role in risk evaluation. Framing the discussion in this manner highlights the important question of how institutional settings—and policymaking functions performed in those settings—affect the use of risk analysis. [1]

A brief statement on the methodology and orientation of the study is necessary. The documentary record provides abundant information on agency and congressional activities concerning risk analysis. To understand the conditions affecting the use of risk analysis, however, that documentary record must be supplemented with data on informal administrative behavior and attitudes of key policy actors in the agencies and on Capitol Hill. To gather such information, semi-structured interviews were conducted in January and in July, 1981 with regulatory agency personnel and congressional staffs. Not all agencies could be covered, but those selected represent a diversity of policy areas and statutory requirements involving risk analysis. [2] This report summarizes the aggregate findings from these interviews, discusses how the use of risk analysis and perceptions of its limitations vary across agencies and across policy areas, and examines the present and potential role of risk analysis both in the agencies and on the Hill. Particular attention is given to the problems in using risk analysis and various needs for improvement cited by the policy actors interviewed. Given the exploratory nature of the research, only qualitative analysis of the interview data is warranted.

RISK ANALYSIS IN THE AGENCIES

Introduction

A wide variety of executive branch agencies are involved with implementation of public policies designed to promote risk reduction. There are some forty major risk control laws presently in force; they are implemented by a great number of agencies. (Kraft, 1982b, Appendices I and III). Many of these policies were enacted or significantly modified in the last 15 years in response to increasing public concern over health, safety and environmental risks. But more recently, regulatory actions in these agencies have generated sharp political conflict because of the costs involved. Industry groups in particular have called for greater use of cost-benefit analysis to force explicit consideration of the costs of compliance. Others with a lesser economic stake in the outcomes have made parallel arguments for using risk analysis and cost-benefit analysis to help set priorities in health, safety and environmental regulation.

Already controversial, implementation of these policies became more sensitive with the issuance of the Reagan Administration's Executive

Order No. 12291 in February, 1981. That order required that cost-benefit analysis be performed for all major proposed rules (those costing $100 million or more annually to implement) in executive agencies. Moreover, agencies were required to choose the least costly alternative or to explain why a more costly one was chosen. The Office of Management and Budget (OMB) was selected as the central coordinating body for review of proposed regulations, and the regulatory review staff from the former Council on Wage and Price Stability (CWPS) was moved to OMB for this purpose. (Its activities and impact are discussed in Viscusi's chapter and in Andrews 1984.)

Whatever the ultimate success of these efforts, one effect of the administration's executive order was clear enough. The use of risk analysis in regulatory decision-making became even more politicized. An interim report by the Task Force on Regulatory Relief (headed by Vice-President George Bush) in early January, 1982 drew immediate criticism from liberals, who accused the administration of damaging public health and safety.[3] And by mid-1983, the Reagan Administration's attempt to weaken implementation of environmental policies (particularly in the area of toxic and hazardous substances) drew so much criticism that it was forced to replace Environmental Protection Agency (EPA) administrator Anne McGill Burford with former administrator William Ruckelshaus. Given this political context, the use of risk analysis in agency decision-making in the near term is inextricably linked to controversies over regulation and regulatory reform. Under such circumstances, separation of the presumably technical task of risk assessment from the political determination of safety (risk evaluation) becomes problematic to say the least. The interview data help to explain why.

Overview of the Findings

Interviews with policymakers and staff professionals in 1981 produced abundant evidence of the pressures to make greater use of risk analysis. Thus while formal risk assessment techniques had not been used very extensively in the past, their use has increased significantly in recent years and is very likely to increase further in the future. Most of those interviewed supported their continued employment, especially when accompanied by further methodological refinements and greater appreciation of their limitations as tools of policy analysis. But attitudes of individual staff and decision-makers toward risk assessment ran the full range from highly positive to strongly negative. The range of perspectives and actions can best be demonstrated with a few illustrations.

The Materials Transportation Bureau (MTB) in the Department of Transportation, for example, has made extensive use of risk assessment, and has contracted for several outside studies in the last few years. But one of its top officials nevertheless expresses some modest doubts about this analytic tool.

> [We have spent] what I would say is a considerable sum on risk analysis studies. . . . Almost every function that we perform here has some sort of risk analysis associated with it. [But] I don't know how to characterize my attitude toward it. Risk analysis is rather a "black art" in some ways.

Supportive statements of this type, even with the reservation noted, were made by the majority of staff and officials interviewed. But some were notably less enthusiastic. A commissioner on the Consumer Product Safety Commission (CPSC), for example, recognized the utility of measuring risk, but was skeptical that it could be done very precisely.

> I personally find risk assessment useful, but not as a major element of a decision. I don't have a lot of faith in it. There's too much uncertainty about the exposure, about mathematical models that are used to make the extrapolations down at the low-dose range . . . .

In all agencies surveyed there was some awareness of the technical limitations of risk analysis, a matter of no little concern to the critics of this methodology (Baram 1982; Bogen 1980). The problems most often mentioned included an inadequate data base (e.g., insufficient epidemiological data), the difficulty of estimating the impact of low-probability but high-consequence hazards, the challenge of analyzing phenomena at the limits of scientific understanding, the measurement of the benefits of risk reduction, and uncertainties in establishing acceptable levels of risk. These problems seem to have been recognized and taken into account by technical staff and by most decisionmakers interviewed. As one biostatistician put it, "I would say people are realistic here. You do the best you can. We're dealing with the best available evidence."

Yet, there was also considerable concern expressed about the potential for misuse of risk analysis by those unfamiliar with such technical limitations. Statutory requirements may force risk-benefit calculations on officials who would otherwise hesitate to make them. And political pressures from Congress and the administration to use risk analysis or cost-benefit analysis in what some officials consider to be an "invalid" manner have been increasing in recent years, as noted above.

Interagency Variation in the Use of Risk Analysis

The extent and type of use of risk analysis varies significantly from agency to agency. This is to be expected given differences in the kind of policy problems dealt with, statutory mandates, organizational characteristics, and attitudes of decision-makers toward risk analysis. Differences in the problems facing each agency are perhaps the most obvious. Some problems are simply more amenable to risk assessment than others. Variables can be more easily identified and controlled, data are available, and the findings can be applied relatively easily. An example is the FDA's assessment of food additives. But consider, in contrast, the task facing the MTB in controlling transportation of hazardous materials:

> You can take isolated pieces of our business and apply risk analysis—specific commodity, specific containment system, specific pathway, and the minute you change any one of those three things, that risk analysis is gone. So what I am dealing with here is not billions, but trillions of permutations. And nobody has shown me the methodology to be applied generally.

Statutory differences are also fairly straightforward. Agencies and policies were created at different times and with varied expectations (Field 1981; Kraft 1982a). Independent agencies operate in a more flexible political environment than those directly accountable to the White House and OMB, a point noted by several officials. And legal constraints on the use of risk assessment (whether required or not, who has the burden of proof, etc.) directly affect decision-making.

Among the agency characteristics that seem to influence the use of analysis are internal capability for performing the technical assessments (primarily having the scientific or technical staff on board), the existence of well established procedures for risk estimation and evaluation, extent of experience with these techniques, and financial resources to support the work. More detailed study of the conditions influencing the extent or type of use of risk assessment should include examination of the comprehensive set of variables generally found to be important in regulatory agencies (Sabatier 1977).

Agency Procedures and the Methodology of Risk Assessment

Given the increasing use of risk assessment in regulatory decision-making it is not surprising that a consensus is developing on the most appropriate methodologies. A number of interagency coordination groups have been established over the past few years and have worked to establish guidelines for the conduct of risk assessments. This type of development is especially evident in the area of carcinogens (Bogen 1981; IRLG 1979). Thus a technical staff person in OSHA reported that:

> we use EPA methodology in a lot of our work. The work has undergone critical review and represents a reasonable state-of-

the-art approach, we feel, to some of these problems. I think there's . . .a consensus on approaches to doing risk assessment.

There is no equivalent consensus for administration procedures in developing standards and regulations. Some agencies have well-defined, formal procedures; others are just beginning to develop them. What is done seems to depend greatly on the particularcase because, as an FDA official put it, "each case presents you with new problems and new opportunities." Typically, however, the risk assessment is performed by a technical or scientific staff, is sent to an office of regulatory analysis where some form of economic analysis is done, and then is sent to the policymakers for a final decision on standards. Unlike the apparently routine work of technical staffs, the regulatory analysis staff is faced with the numerous uncertainties involved in risk evaluation, especially in the calculation of costs and benefits of regulation. President Reagan's 1981 executive order on cost-benefit analysis in the agencies represented a major effort to bring some consistency to these procedures. At this writing, however, there is still considerable variation in agency methods of risk evaluation and in the procedures followed after the technical job of risk estimation.

To judge from the interviews, most agencies have adapted to the inherent limitations of risk analysis and to the political context in which regulatory policy operates by developing informal procedures. In OSHA, for example, the regulatory analysis office reports are "not a one shot deal (but result from) an iterative process," involving repeated discussions with the political officials and multiple studies and draft reports. In the FDA, there is usually "a collaborative effort between the scientists, on the one hand, and the consumer safety officers on the other. They work it out in a collaborative, cooperative way." When the reports reach the Commissioner's office, the dialogue continues, with sharp questioning of the science, the legal implications, and the consistency of judgments made.

> The reason you need all of this interaction between science and policy . . .to come to a regulatory decision is that because of the softness, because of the uncertainty, we cannot, should not, be capricious. And if you just left the technical people to their own devices, they can, unwittingly, be quite capricious. Because they are not the guardians of the overall process, that assures some degree of consistency.

These kinds of procedural adaptations seem particularly significant in light of extensive criticisms of the methodological inadequacies of risk analysis. They help to minimize the use of poor analysis or poor data by subjecting the risk estimation and economic analyses to scrutiny by a diverse set of participants. Maintenance of such a pluralistic decisionmaking process seems to be an important characteristic of several of the more "successful" agencies.

Methodological Improvements

Despite the constraints noted above, improvements in methodologies will likely produce greater use of risk assessment across a broad range of policy problems. The interviews elicited several noteworthy suggestions for such improvements, including ways of dealing with uncertainty and how to present it, expansion of data bases, the level of specificity of the assessments, the format in which studies are presented, and consistency in risk evaluation methods. Space here allows only a few brief comments, but additional suggestions emanating from the congressional interviews are presented below.

Most of those who work with risk assessment would endorse the need for expanded data bases, but a special effort needs to be made to develop them. As an OSHA administrator noted, there is a need to create incentives for doing so.

> Most people in high levels of public service have a fairly short-term horizon . . .and many of them object to developing long-term kinds of data bases . . .which may not be of much benefit to the current generation of decision-makers.

The specificity or concreteness of a risk assessment is also important. Excessively general risk analyses were dismissed by one official in the MTB as essentially worthless, whereas one that ''really worked'' addressed specific questions the office had to face and presented the material in readable and direct English rather than in technical jargon. Similarly, a technical official at the Nuclear Regulatory Commission (NRC) noted a case in which the Commission ''used [the] risk assessment in a decision, clearly and explicitly.'' It was one that the Commission requested the staff to prepare in ''just a few weeks'' on a particular plant. It was done quickly and was geared to answer the specific questions posed. The lesson seems to be that to facilitate direct utilization of risk assessment, there is a need to understand, as an Interior Department official put it, ''what it is that people who are making policy need to have in order to feel comfortable in decisions.'' While these examples do not imply that a single approach or style is appropriate for all risk analyses, they do suggest a need to improve institutional capabilities for performing specific risk analyses quickly and cheaply. They also suggest the importance of using a language, style, and format suitable for a policymaking audience of nonspecialists.

Consistency in risk evaluation methods was not mentioned as frequently as other problems, but is clearly an area in need of improvement. Consider the following statement by an official at the NRC:

Most regulators make decisions in a fashion that's quite similar. Information is put on the table, technical information, and the regulator looks at it, circles the table three times, and casts a judgment column on the table. And that's a regulatory decision. And then the regulator tries to defend that decision through a hearing process or a public comment process or whatever the regulator has to do. The real issue is what's the information you put on the table and how do you sort it out? Because in the last analysis it does boil down to judgment. In any complex regulatory field no simple formula will suffice.

This perspective is an important reminder that most of the professional commentary on risk analysis concerns technical issues of risk identification and risk estimation. Much less attention has been given to the manner in which judgments are made about the acceptability of risk. This omission is particularly striking because it is the supposed arbitrary or biased process of determining the public interest in these matters that provokes so much dissent about governmental regulation in the 1980s. An examination of congressional involvement with risk analysis should be especially instructive on these critical and largely ignored processes of risk evaluation.

RISK ANALYSIS IN CONGRESS

Introduction

Most discussions of risk analysis in regulation focus on administrative agencies. Although this focus is understandable, federal agencies are implementing policies enacted by the Congress exercising its constitutional lawmaking powers. Most of these policies of necessity give considerable discretion to the agencies to determine appropriate standards and regulations. As a consequence of the controversies that have arisen over agency decision-making and the use of risk assessment, Congress in recent years has taken a serious interest in the subject. That interest can best be described as part of a more general concern with regulatory reform. But legislation has also been introduced to improve the methodologies and applications of risk assessment through research and demonstration projects; and numerous oversight hearings have been held in the last several years in response to decisions of the Reagan Administration. Because Congress has the legal authority to alter public policies governing agency activities and can influence agency actions through oversight hearings and budgetary decisions, it is obviously an important institution shaping the future of risk analysis.

For present purposes, one might add that Congress is especially important because it is the most representative branch of government. It is also a strong and independent institution capable of challenging the executive branch, and often more friendly to interests ignored by the administration. In the early 1980s, for example, consumer and environmental groups found Congress much more receptive to their arguments than was the Reagan Administration. If technical expertise lies in the agencies and legal expertise in the courts, Congress can lay claim to political expertise in the best sense of that term. A major challenge of modern government is to make policy choices that are responsive to public demands or needs as well as "correct" technically; and Congress is the institution best suited for keeping government accountable to the public, if not necessarily for ensuring that public policy is always coherent or economically efficient. The use of risk analysis in the legislative process should be assessed with those needs in mind.

The Major Issues

In contrast to the fairly well-defined role of risk analysis in the agencies, there is no agreement on the way in which risk analysis is used or ought to be used in the legislative process. The lack of consensus was evident in a major set of hearings held in July, 1979 (U.S. Congress 1980). Many of the problems with risk analysis identified there parallel those noted in the agency interviews. Among other significant problems or issues raised were: the poor understanding of risk on the part of the general public; the inadequate coverage of risk-related events, probabilistic concepts, and conflicting scientific claims by the media; and the most appropriate role for Congress in risk-benefit analysis. Regarding the last, there were two sharply contrasting views: (1) that Congress should *not* be involved in the day-to-day or routine decisions of risk management, but should limit its actions to setting policies and criteria for evaluating the acceptability of risk (that is, the more political decisions); (2) that risk-benefit analysis is too subjective to leave solely to agencies and reputed "experts," and therefore that members of Congress should play a much *expanded* role as the legitimate representatives of the American public.

The present study, of course, was designed in part to provide reliable, if tentative, information about the present degree of interest in risk analysis on the Hill, the prevailing perspectives toward its employment in regulation, and problems and needs in congressional use of risk analyses. The role that Congress ought to play is a matter of political preference or judgment about relative institutional capacities. But some of the information presented below may bear on those preferences and judgments.

Congressional Interest in Risk Analysis

In a review of risk analysis in the U.S. Congress, Moss and Lubin

(1981) report that "risk analysis *is* part of the legislative process and is being used all the time, in a great variety of ways." Certainly, one can find corroborative evidence for the assertion in the range of committees with formal legislative or oversight responsibility involving risk analysis (see Hadden's introduction), and in the number and variety of congressional hearings and studies in the past few years (Kraft, 1982a; U.S. Congress 1980c). Yet productive legislative activity in the committee roomsdoes not necessarily indicate widespread interest among the general membership of Congress nor appreciable understanding of the technical difficulties in conducting risk assessments. Interviews with House and Senate committee staff as well as with staff of the Office of Technology Assessment (OTA) and the Congressional Research Service (CRS), confirm those suspicions.

For example, according to a senior staff member of the Science Policy Division in CRS, the basis of current interest in risk analysis is largely the politicization of the regulatory reform movement; members and their staffs believe they need to cover themselves by keeping abreast of any new developments in the area, but they have little interest in probing deeply. Consequently, he said, they have little understanding of the complex methods of generating risk assessments, the uncertainties involved, and scientific disagreements.

These conclusions lead to a somewhat complex answer to the question of congressional interest and involvement in risk analysis. To judge from the activities of key committees and the more technically sophisticated members, risk analysis is solidly on the congressional agenda; Congress is deeply involved and likely to play a major role in the future. At the same time, the majority of members remain only marginally interested; their role in any future risk policy activities is more difficult to predict. There are some important implications for what Congress needs to know about technological risks and risk assessment methods.

Problems Identified by Congressional Staff and Suggested Improvements

Interviews with Congressional staff substantially reinforced the general picture presented in the joint hearings. Some of the technical limitations were underscored and additional problems of a political and organizational nature were mentioned. Some of the more significant comments merit review here. They will be presented under three categories: methodology, available resources, and institutional capacity.

Methodology.

Nearly all individuals interviewed on the Hill noted the general difficulty in performing risk analysis, mentioning one or more of the technical limitations discussed earlier. As one division director of the OTA put it, the problems addressed are often complex and too difficult to analyze, and scientists are not always equipped to answer the kind of questions posed by members of Congress. Congressmen often say "give me a number;" they have relatively less interest in the methods used to reach conclusions than in the "bottom line" of the study. A staff member in the CRS noted, similarly, that scientific capabilities are "not high," and that this was not understood by most members of Congress. Thus, there is often a conflict between politicians eager to identify, measure and mitigate risks—in order to respond to public demands to "do something" about the risks—and the scientists who must perform the assessments (also see National Research Council 1982).

The complex nature of risk analysis, limited scientific capability, and the production of varying estimates of risk lead congressional staff and the technical advisors in OTA and CRS to one of two distinct positions: (1) that present methodology is inadequate and must be improved before risk assessments can be of much use to Congress; or (2) that scientists must learn how to work with the present limited capabilities and should not wait for improved methodologies. The first position is characteristic of "scientific purists" who are more removed from the day-to-day decision-making on the Hill. They tend to invoke professional standards and to speak critically of "premature" application of risk assessment methodologies. The second position was more common in the group interviewed. It reflects the position of those staffers more sympathetic to the need of members of Congress to act in the short term than to the protestations of scientific staff that more research and methodological improvements are necessary before any advice can be rendered. Thus what members need most, said one division director at OTA, is a kind of "macro-risk analysis" to allow them to "rationalize policy decisions" in order to explain to their constituents the basic for their actions.

Resources

In a recent review of environmental risk analysis, Moss noted that the nation lacks the resources necessary to gather and analyze comprehensive data on a wide range of environmental problems. If legislatures insist on "airtight arguments" to make decisions, he said, scientific resources will be severely strained; the cost of data gathering and analysis "may be staggering" (Moss, 1980). His observations were echoed by many of the professional staff interviewed. For example, according to a program director at OTA, the amount of money available to conduct the studies is simply not sufficient to answer the questions put to OTA by members of Congress. He added, "there is not likely to be any significant improvement in that picture anytime soon.

What is needed for the future? There is no easy answer. Some call for substantially greater investment in research and training programs to improve scientific capabilities for performing detailed risk assessments.

They believe only such scientifically valid studies will suffice, given the sharp political conflict surrounding the major regulatory issues. But others suggest that limited budgetary resources can be invested with a greater return if the scientific community gives more emphasis to economical ways of performing risk assessments. Members of Congress and interested parties would have to settle for less definitive answers to technical questions, but might make more progress in setting policy if they reach agreement on what methodologies would be acceptable for such purposes.

Institutional Capacity

Congress is often criticized for its institutional weaknesses. Overlapping committee jurisdictions, limited capacity for highly technical policy analysis, vulnerabilty to pressure from a range of narrow interest groups, and a tendency toward short-term and palliative solutions to policy problems are commonly noted. Similar arguments were made in the interviews. Two other major constraints on producing and using risk analyses deserve mention. Several high-level staffers in OTA and CRS emphasized the lack of an institutional mechanism for bringing together the scientific community and the decision-makers. As one director in CRS put it, there is much ignorance and uncertainty in Congress on risk assessment, but scientists are not well-equipped by themselves to improve the situation. The two sides reflect different professional training and perspectives, respond to different concerns, and often speak different languages. While he is "not quite sure why," he believes CRS and OTA cannot resolve this problem by themselves.

A second limitation is that congressional oversight of agency activities tends to be unsystematic and uncoordinated, and occurs irregularly. Investigations and oversight depend heavily on the motivation of senior committee members, available staff resources, and the expected visibility and political appeal of the proceedings (Aberbach 1980; Ogul 1976). Moreover, Congress is strongly supportive of much bureaucratic activity; committees or subcommittees which might otherwise be expected to provide oversight and criticism are instead closely tied to the particular "sub-government" involved.

What might be done to improve institutional capacity? There has never been a shortage of recommendations for reforming Congress, and a number of the standard prescriptions are relevant for improving use of risk analysis. These include clarification of committee jurisdictions, provision of greater incentives and resources for oversight of administrative agencies, and enhancement of capacity for technical policy analysis. Perhaps the greatest need is for a mechanism or process for improving congressional understanding of the scientific issues in risk analysis. Much depends on the scientific community itself and its willingness and ability to inform members of Congress and the public on technological risks. Those interviewed emphasized development of new ways of communicating with the public and with Congress, particularly for sorting out conflicting scientific claims and for presenting probabilistic concepts.

Comparing Congress and the Agencies

How does the use of risk analysis in Congress compare with its use in the agencies? And how might that change if Congress assumes one or another of the two roles identified earlier: more direct involvement in agency decisions of risk management through extensive use of its oversight functions, or more limited involvement, with emphasis on clarifying policies and criteria for evaluating risks? The first question can be answered through use of the interview data, but the second calls for some speculation on the institutional and political implications of the two roles.

For the most part, the use of risk analysis in these two quite different institutional settings is what one would expect given the characteristics and functions of the agencies on the one hand and Congress on the other. The former are highly specialized bureaucratic organizations staffed with technical and policy experts. They deal with a relatively narrow constituency of knowledgeable individuals who demand well-developed and articulated rationales for agency decisions. Risk assessment is seen as a technical, if imperfect, methodology for providing information necessary for such decisions. Although the highest-level policy staffs are concerned with the more political processes of risk evaluation (particularly when subject to central review by the OMB), the agencies follow a well-defined procedure for developing and using technical information, and seek to defend agency decisions chiefly on those grounds. This is not to say that economic and political forces have no influence on regulatory decision-making; obviously they are extremely important (Wilson 1980). But agency decisions are also subject to judicial review and thus must be based on defensible interpretations of statutes and acceptable evidence and methods of analysis (Vig, this volume). Lave (1983) puts it well:

> A careful review of scientific evidence and a quantitative risk assessment should be the basis of regulatory decisions. Regulation without these elements is uniformed, arbitrary, and unlikely to withstand litigation, induce cooperation from those being regulated, or produce the results desired.

In contrast Congress is an independent, intensely political and highly fragmented organization. Decision-making authority on risk policies is dispersed among dozens of committees and subcommittees, making coordination of policies and consistency in evaluative criteria unlikely. Most members of Congress, including many on those committees, have little background in science and technology and pay little attention to the issues in risk policy. The general public they represent tends to misperceive and overreact to technological risks, but is ambivalent about safety and the cost of government regulation to that end (Harris 1980). Congress mirrors both the poor understanding of risks and the ambivalence over regulation. Members expect risk analysis to clarify the political choices they face and to provide a partial rationale for their decisions. But there are no well-defined procedures for developing and using risk analyses—even in the relevant committees and subcommittees, nor do members defend their decisions mainly on technical grounds. Given the adversarial nature of the political process and their lack of scientific training, members often discount the scientific basis of regulatory decisions and stress legalistic standards of evidence, ideological values, the economic interests of particular industries or groups affected by regulatory decisions, or general public fears over health and safety.

In short, the use of risk analysis in the legislative process is affected not only by technical weaknesses in methodologies, but by the very nature of decision-making in Congress. Members of Congress believe that ''good public policy'' emerges from a process of extended debate and deliberation that allows for a full airing of public and interest group concerns. They are not willing to rely solely on the analyses performed by scientific and professional experts in the agencies. In effect, Congress adds a strong measure of political rationality to the bureaucratic standard of technical rationality.

Can Congress play a more active role in the regulation of technological risks? Is public policy on risk likely to be improved if it does so? In terms of institutional capacity there are few major impediments to a more active congressional role in risk analysis. If the problems and needs identified above are attended to, Congress is probably capable of a good deal more involvement with regulatory actions in the agencies. There is more disagreement about whether assumption of such a role is desirable. Political scientists frequently have advocated a much greater oversight role for Congress in the belief that the oversight function is a particularly suitable one for representative legislatures (Huntington 1973; Aberbach 1980). As noted above, greater congressional supervision of agency use of risk analysis might bring a more democratic perspective to what tends otherwise to be technocratic decision-making; certainly public fears about risks would be more likely to be given consideration. And significant biases or procedural irregulaties in the agencies would be less likely to occur if a strong, independent congressional presence were assured. But other scholars and many scientists have argued that risk assessment belongs in the agencies and not in Congress. They believe public policy would not be improved through increased congressional oversight, partly because the direction and impact of that oversight may be affected by political pressure from well-organized interest groups and because members are too poorly informed to understand the scientific basis for agency actions. Instead they would have Congress limit its actions to reducing inconsistency in statutory mandates for risk assessments and clarifying evaluative criteria to guide agency decisionmaking.

No one really knows, of course, precisely how use of risk analysis would change if Congress assumes a more active role. But regardless of preference for one kind of institutional decision-making or another, it seems clear that Congress will necessarily be involved when agencies consider or adopt health, safety and environmental regulations having a significant impact on the American public. Moss and Lubin (1981) explain why:

> We can't turn back the clock of political mood. We can't tell legislative bodies that they will have to wait for better science, or better risk assessment methodology, or better-risk balancing institutions (mechanisms) to develop from the better science.

Rather than debate the merits of variable congressional or agency roles, one might better assume that Congress has certain political needs that must be met and proceed to develop the institutional capacity that will allow Congress to participate in regulation of technological risks. To do otherwise is to invite continuous controversy and regulatory stalemate.

Development of such an institutional capacity is no easy trick. The internal dynamics and organization of Congress militate against efficient or coordinated approaches to risk policy, and in general there are to many policy issues, too many competing demands for scarce resources and too little time for members to make risk policy a high priority item on the congressional agenda. But the kind of risk analysis that Congress needs should be clear enough from the interview data and discussion above. It is not going to use risk analysis the way the agencies do and does not need to have the expansive research base that scientific "purists" typically advocate. Members do need to understand the basis of agency decisions, however, and be able to separate out the factual elements in risk analysis from the judgmental. To provide such information to Congress, the scientific community and agency decision-makers need to develop more flexible methods of risk analysis and to learn how to communicate methods and findings to members more clearly. Experimenting with a diversity of approaches should provide some evidence on what kind of information and what kind of procedural arrangements are likely to be most effective toward these ends.

CONCLUSION

Risk analysis techniques are not now and will not ever be a panacea for dealing with the multiple hazards of modern industrial societies. Even if methods of risk estimation are further refined and other limitations on their use are overcome, there will remain the subjective element inherent in evaluating risks and devising appropriate public policies or regulations. But risk assessment methodologies can be useful tools of policy analysis if employed carefully, experimentally, and with proper regard for the uncertainty of scientific knowledge.

Given the problems noted by agency personnel and congressional staff, and the political nature of judging what is "safe," among the issues meriting study by political scientists and other policy scholars are where, how, and by whom risk evaluations should be performed (Nelkin and Pollack 1980). What are the respective and legitimate roles for professional staffs in the agencies and on the Hill, the scientific community, appointed officials, and elected decision-makers? What should be the role for the public at large? How do present capabilities compare with those called for by these roles? What new capabilities are needed? What new institutional mechanisms might facilitate "better" decision-making on technological risks?

Some of the findings reported in this chapter and others in the book bear on such questions. But much more systematic study is necessary to determine the conditions for successful performance of risk assessments and risk evaluations within regulatory agencies and the conditions for effective policymaking and oversight by the Congress. Empirical studies of factors influencing the present conduct, use and impact of risk analysis in the agencies and on Capitol Hill would be especially desirable. They might provide valuable guidelines both for improving risk assessment methodologies and for productive changes in the processes of risk evaluation.

NOTES

1.   Research for this work was supported by a grant from the National Science Foundation, Division of Policy Research and Analysis, NSF PRA 800 7228. The chapter is based largely on two reports prepared for the J. H. Wiggins Company under the NSF grant (Kraft 1982a and 1982b). The larger study of which this is a part is "An Integrated Analysis of Risk Assessment Methodologies and Their Employment in Governmental Risk Management Decisionmaking," Lloyd L. Philipson and Arthur A. Atkisson, co-principal investigators. Opinions and conclusions stated here do not necessarily represent the views of the co-principal investigators or the National Science Foundation.

2.   The agencies covered in the study included the following: the Nuclear Regulatory Commission, the Occupational Safety and Health Administration, the Food and Drug Administration, the Consumer Product Safety Commission, the Environmental Protection Agency, the Materials Transportation Bureau of the Department of Transportation, and the Office of Minerals and Energy of the Department of the Interior. Interviews were also conducted with professional staffs in the Regulatory Council, the Office of Management and Budget, the Council on Environmental Quality, and selected congressional committees and policy advisory bodies. The most important in the last category were the General Accounting Office, the Office of Technology Assessment, and the Congressional Research Service. Within each agency, office, committee or advisory body, individuals were selected for interviews based on several criteria: formal positions held in offices responsible for risk assessment or regulatory analysis, membership on the national Academy of Science—National Science Foundation Risk Analysis Liaison Committee, and/or reputation for extensive involvement with risk analysis. This is a group familiar with the methodologies of risk assessment and knowledgeable about agency and congressional procedures regarding its use. Most interviews were recorded, allowing excerpts from the transcripts to be used here.

3.   This is recounted in *Newsweek*, January 11, 1982.

Chapter 3

AUTOMOBILE CRASH PROTECTION: INSTITUTIONAL RESPONSES TO SELF-HAZARDOUS BEHAVIOR
John D. Graham[1]

Editor's Introduction

While many of the risk-benefit analyses discussed by Kraft's respondents have been kept as internal agency documents, some are more widely available. The earlier version of this symposium included an exemplary, if simplified, risk-benefit analysis of asbestos in government buildings (Dyer, 1982). Graham's paper serves several different purposes in this volume, one of which is to provide the reader with an introduction to the kinds of calculations he might find in a full-blown risk-benefit analysis. Table 1 of his paper and its associated text only hint at the complexity of the underlying calculations.

Graham's paper adds to our understanding of present institutional arrangements for controlling risk by describing a policy area in which there are not only a multiplicity of actors but a multiplicity of policy choices, each of which entails a different balance of power among those actors. Especially important is his explicit discussion of the institutional needs of the nongovernmental actors—in this case, of automobile dealers prevented for perfectly rational reasons from allowing increased safety to become a selling point for their vehicles.

The marketplace is a nongovernmental institution that can be used to control risks; its advantage is, of course, that the market allows individuals to obtain different amounts of risk prevention according to their preferences. One of the most striking features of Graham's paper is the tension he highlights between our general preference for relying on the market and the inability of the market to provide an acceptable level of automobile safety in view of drivers' irrationality of ignorance. This tension results in hostility to a government that acts to provide the electorate with "what they really want, not what they think they want," and may compromise governmental institutions unrelated to those involved in the particular regulatory effort in question. Rosenbaum's paper in this volume explores this question as well.

INTRODUCTION

In 1966 Congress passed the National Traffic and Motor Vehicle Safety Act. The federal government was authorized to establish safety standards for all new cars sold in the United States. Sponsors of the legislation hoped that the legal mandate and subsequent regulatory action would stimulate new car designs with superior crash-protection features.

As a result of the 1966 Act, some progress has been made. Most cars on the road are now equipped with padded dashboards, collapsible steering columns, penetration-resistant windshields, head restraints, side-door reinforcements, lap and shoulder belts and other safety features. Many of these design changes, required by regulation in the late 1960s, have been shown to be effective in reducing the chances of occupant injury in a crash. For example, the probability of death and serious injury to occupants is 25 to 35 percent less for cars subject to federal regulation than for unregulated cars.[2] Almost all of this improvement is accounted for by safety features adopted before 1970. The General Accounting Office (GAO) found no evidence of subsequent improvement in the crashworthiness of cars in the early 1970s.

The need for enhanced occupant-crash protection has not subsided. In 1980 approximately 27,500 passenger car occupants in the United States were killed in highway accidents. Another 500,000 occupants suffered nonfatal injuries ranging in severity from a broken nose to permanent spinal cord injury. Automobile accidents are the leading cause of death among people from the age of one year to 35 years and a major cause of paraplegia and epilepsy. These facts highlight the large number of high quality life-years that are harmed or destroyed by car crashes.

A persistent problem preventing further improvement in occupant-crash protection has been the low rate of use of safety belts. Despite over a decade of political debate in Congress, state legislatures, the courts, and the Department of Transportation, no progress has been made toward saving lives with occupant-restraint systems. In fact, the rate of safety belt use actually declined several percentage points in the late 1970s to a low of 11.8 percent in 1980 (Opinion Research Corp. 1980).

Several administrators of the National Highway Traffic Safety Administration (NHTSA) initiated rulemaking to require installation of passive restraints in all new cars (i.e., air bags or automatic safety belts). The regulatory efforts have had minimal effect. Less than one percent of all new cars sold in the United States since model year 1974 have been equipped with any kind of passive restraint system (Graham, Henrion, and Morgan 1981).

The purpose of this paper is to think through the policy questions raised by the lack of adequate occupant-crash protection. Parts I and II establish the need for government policy by exposing deficiencies in the decision-making of motorists, car purchasers, and automobile manufacturers. In Part III some policy directions are proposed that can save lives yet not instigate the vocal political opposition that has plagued previous initiatives. A major theme of the paper is that government decision-makers should design auto safety policy to minimize the probability and adverse consequences of public opposition which is inevitable when government attempts to regulate areas which appear to be amenable to individual decisionmaking. The hostility can endanger regulatory efforts in many areas other than the one at issue.

I. BELT-USE DECISON-MAKING

A person's decision about whether to buckle his or her safety belt can be modeled as a benefit-cost judgment. On the benefit side are the reduced chances of serious injury and death and resulting financial benefits. The "costs" of belt use are more amorphous, but they include the time and mental energy consumed in deciding whether to buckle up, the time and inconvenience associated with the act of buckling up, the discomfort of being strapped in a seat and, perhaps, the unpleasantness of being reminded that one is vulnerable to crash injury. The model predicts that a motorist will buckle up if the perceived safety benefits exceed the "costs" of buckling up.

Several economists have argued that it may be rational for the average motorist to decide against buckling up (Thaler and Rosen 1975; Blomquist and Pelzman 1981). Some rough calculations shed light on the issue. The average driver's chances of being killed in a car accident are about 1.4 in 10,000 per year. The corresponding chances of moderate-to-severe nonfatal injury are 25 in 10,000 per year. Safety experts estimate that lap-shoulder belts can (if worn) reduce a driver's chances of death and serious injury in a crash by 30 to 70 percent. Thus, the economic benefit of belt use can be estimated under various assumptions about how much money people might be willing to pay for extra safety.

Benefit estimates for belt use are presented in Table 1. The estimates range from $25 to $200 per year depending upon two uncertain variables: the effectiveness of belts in reducing injury and the motorist's willingness to pay for safety. Since the decision to buckle up is sometimes made on a per trip basis, it is useful to express safety benefits in these units. The average driver makes about 780 trips per year so the benefits of buckling up are 3 to 25 cents per trip.

Table 1
Estimated Annual Benefit of Safety Belt Usage for the Average Driver

Valuation Assumptions	Belt Effectiveness Assumptions		
	30%	50%	70%
1. $500,000/fatality $5,000/injury	$24.75	$ 41.25	$ 57.75
2. $2.0 million/fatality $20,000/injury	$57.00	$ 95.00	$148.70
3. $1.5 million/fatality $30,000/injury	$85.50	$142.50	$199.50

Notes: The average driver's annual probability of death in a car crash is 0.00014. Calculated as 20,330 driver deaths (1979) divided by 143 million licensed drivers. The corresponding probability of nonfatal injury is 0.0025 per year.

Source: *Highway Safety,* Annual Report, National Highway Traffic Safety Administration, Washington, D.C., 1979, A–17.

The issue boils down to the following: Are the modest inconveniences and discomforts of manual belt usage sufficient to forego a financial payment of $25–200 per driver per year? Some drivers will rationally turn down the financial gain, particularly for the lower end of the payment range. But it is difficult to believe that 80–90 percent of drivers perceive the ''costs'' of belt usage to be that substantial. Many people may not be behaving rationally (i.e., according to their own interest). The optimal voluntary belt usage rate (assuming perfectly rational decision-making) is probably higher than 10 percent, possibly as high as 60–70 percent. It is surely not 90–100 percent, however, since some motorists have very low objective risks of crash involvement, have special aversions to discomfort, and/or have low preferences for safety. It is impossible to prove that most motorists are behaving irrationally, but some circumstantial evidence suggests that ill-informed and inconsistent behavior is widespread.

Variability in Belt-Use Rates

If the belt-use habits of motorists are based on well-informed, rational decision-making, one might expect observed usage rates to vary considerably depending upon factors relevant to a benefit-cost assessment. For example, belt-use rates should be higher in driving conditions known to be hazardous.

For several years NHTSA has funded large-scale, national observational surveys of the shoulder-belt usage habits of drivers. These surveys, along with studies conducted by independent investigators, have established that belt-use rates are not uniformly distributed. Although the average observed national usage rate on all roads fluctuates between 10 – 15 percent, it appears that 20 to 40 percent of Americans wear safety belts on certain occasions. Differences in belt-use rates provide an opportunity to examine the decisionmaking of motorists.

Data on belt use, summarized in Table 2, reveal some puzzling patterns. One factor has an unequivocally positive effect on belt use: length of trip.

Table 2
Data on Patterns of Safety Belt Use

Attribute of Road, Trip, Vehicle or Occupant	Anticipated Effect on Belt-Use Rate	Actual Effect on Belt Usage	Source
Time of Day and Week	Usage rates should be higher on weekends and/or nights when serious accidents occur	No statistical association	ORC (1980)
Rural vs. Urban Roads	Usage rates should be higher on rural roads where risk of fatal accident per mile is 60 percent higher	Usage rates *lower* on rural roads than on urban roads	ORC (1980)
Size of Car	Usage rates should be highest in small cars due to greater injury risk	No statistical association	(O'Neill, et al., 1983)
Occupant Seating	Usage rates should be higher for front-right passenger than driver due to greater injury risk	Usage rates *lower* for front-right passenger than driver	(Ricci, 1979)
Length of Trip	Usage rates should be higher on long trips	Reported usage rates twice as high for long vs. short trips	(Blomquist and Peltzman, 1981)

This finding lends some credence to the rationality hypothesis: it makes some sense to buckle up once for, say, two hours (120 miles) of protection than to buckle up once for 20 minutes (20 miles of protection). The fixed "cost" of buckling up is spread over a longer period of benefit stream, thus increasing the motorist's incentive to opt for protection.

Since the data on variability in belt use present such a mixed story, good multi-variate analysis of belt-use patterns is needed. Perhaps the most striking fact is that 60−80 percent of motorists *never* wear safety belts, regardless of the length of trip, type of vehicle, or road conditions. The persistence of unbelted behavior can only be explained in two ways: (1) the "disutilities" of belt use overwhelm the safety benefits to motorists, regardless of driving conditions; or (2) there are systematic deficiencies in the decision-making of motorists that cause behavior inconsistent with the rational model. Given the limited nature of belt-use costs and the wide range of dangers in different driving conditions, the first explanation seems implausible (though it cannot be refuted). There is some supplementary evidence consistent with the second explanation.

The Psychology of Small Probabilities

Psychological research indicates that people have difficulty comprehending events with low probabilities and highly adverse consequences (Kahneman, Slovic, and Tversky 1982). A motorist's reluctance to wear safety belts may reflect a general tendency of people to ignore events with very small probabilities, regardless of the consequences (Arnould and Grabowski 1981). The cognitive task is complicated further since a belt system cannot eliminate the risk of injury and death, it can only reduce the risk. Few motorists are likely to have a good grasp of either the probabilities of accident involvement or the percentage effectiveness of safety belts. Thus, even if the safety benefits of belt-use exceed the usage costs, people may travel unbelted simply because they are unable to process information about highly improbable events.

Compounding the problem posed by small probabilities is a psychological barrier to personal health practices witnessed frequently by students of public health. Whether the risk is cancer, heart disease or car accidents, people have a tendency to deny their own vulnerabilities to death and illness. Underestimation of accident risk appears to be prevalent (Robertson 1977). In one survey of 1,500 licensed drivers, only 23 percent of respondents chose probabilities of being in an accident equal to or greater than the national average (Teknekron 1979). The "it-won't-happen-to-me" attitude appears to be prevalent in people's thinking about car accidents.

There is generally a major difference between a person's assessment of the national highway safety problem and that same person's assessment of personal vulnerability to highway accidents. Opinion surveys reveal that a majority of Americans are supportive of corporate and governmental efforts to save lives on the highway, but this societal concern does not manifest itself in personal vulnerability to highway accidents. (Lund and Williams 1982).

This is but another example of what appears to be a pervasive irrationality in individual response to the risks of driving, an irrationality that characterizes other risk decisions as well and raises serious questions of policy. In short, social institutions must decide whether they have a responsibility to foster safety-regarding actions by individuals when those individuals have, under conditions of free choice, exhibited no inclination to do so. While experts have often stated that there is such a responsibility, especially in light of people's inabilities to understand and use probabilistic information (see references in Hadden, this volume), a decision to undertake social risk control programs poses risks to the institutions involved. If people have chosen not to control a risk, they may well resent government interference; the fact that government has taken action may also increase people's anxieties by appearing to signal a greater risk than really exists. These issues are discussed in more detail in an examination of other policy options.

II. PASSIVE RESTRAINTS AND THE AUTOMOTIVE MARKET

A technological alternative to manual safety belts is some type of passive-restraint system. A consensus of technical evidence indicates that air bags (with or without use of a lap belt) and automatic safety belts (if not disconnected) could reduce an occupant's chances of death and serious injury in a crash by at least 25 percent and possibly by as much as the manual 3-point belt system. Safety advocates argue that many consumers would be willing to pay extra for air bags and automatic safety belts, but the auto manufacturers have been ''withholding'' these safety features from the market. The argument requires some evaluation.

Surveying Consumers

Marketing surveys have shown some latent consumer demand for passive restraints. For instance, in 1971 General Motors Corporation asked 630 new car buyers to participate in a brief workshop on the operation, cost and benefits of air bags. A follow-up survey found that 50 percent of the purchasers preferred air bags over a choice between manual belts or no restraints. More recent General Motors marketing surveys in 1978 and 1979 found substantial consumer demand for air bags, even at a price of $360 (1980 dollars).

The automatic safety belt also appears to have a potential constituency among new car buyers. If air bags were priced at $350 above the price of automatic belts, 50 percent of respondents in one survey preferred automatic belts, 35 percent preferred air bags and the remainder preferred neither system. If air bags are only $200 more expensive than automatic belts, 44 percent prefer air bags, 41 percent prefer automatic belts and the remainder prefer neither system. The survey, based on 2,016 home interviews in May, 1978, suggests that significant numbers of car buyers would be willing to pay the extra costs of passive restraints (Hart 1978).

Findings from marketing surveys should be greeted with some skepticism. Most new products introduced in the United States are backed by persuasive marketing evidence, but many of these products fail to survive a year in the market. People are often more willing to pay for product improvements with their words than with their wallets. In any event, the stated preferences of consumers are likely to be volatile since few people know very much about passive restraints.

Passive Restraints in the Market

Real-world marketing experience with passive restraints has been limited yet not negligible. General Motors is the only manufacturer to offer air bags on a significant basis. During model years 1974−76, air bags were offered as a $200−300 option (1974 dollars) on several of General Motors' full-size car lines. Despite a production capacity of 100,000 units in each of the three years, only 10,000 cars were sold with air bags. The lack of sales is somewhat remarkable since the air bag was competing against the unpopular starter-interlock system during its first year as an option (model year 1974). General Motors terminated the air bag program in 1977 due to a lack of consumer demand.

Former General Motors President, Ed Cole, was clearly enthusiastic about the optional air bag program and some effort was made to sell the air bag. General Motors dealers were provided with movies of air-bag crash performance to be shown to prospective customers. Eighteen city newspapers and several national news magazines were targeted with advertisements promoting the air bag. Yet there is good reason to believe that Cole's enthusiasm for the air bag was not communicated effectively to dealers and consumers.

General Motors commissioned a follow-up survey of car owners who could have purchased an optional air bag. One-fourth of the buyers were "very much aware" of the air cushion option, but one-third of the buyers "had not the slightest notion" that there was an air bag option. The $300 price (1974 dollars) was cited as a significant deterrent to sales. About one-third of the buyers said they would have purchased the air bag at a price of $200 (1974 dollars). On the basis of the survey a General Motors official wrote:

. . .General Motors car buyers still remain rather ignorant of air cushion fundamentals and benefits and therefore have not developed any conscious ''need'' for such a system that might compel them to buy it despite its price (Lundstrom, 1975).

Marketing evidence with automatic belts is more extensive and the record mixed. Following disappointing sales of a two-point automatic belt, the Chevette was equipped with a new 3-point nondetachable belt system for model year 1980. About $1.5 million was spent on promotional efforts. The new belt system was offered as a zero-cost option for most of the model year and a $25 bonus was provided to dealers for each car sold with automatic belts. The sales record was nonetheless dismal. Although the Chevette was in high demand during model year 1980, only 3 percent of the 415,000 cars sold were equipped with automatic belts. Volkswagen has achieved more success selling cars with passive belts. The company is now offering a 2-point passive belt with knee pads as a $50 option on the custom Rabbit and as standard equipment on the deluxe Rabbit. During the past seven model years (1976−82) roughly 400,000 Rabbits have been sold with automatic belts. The only other manufacturer to offer passive belts was Toyota. An expensive ($350) motorized belt system is standard equipment on a luxury model (the Cressida) with limited sales. A NHTSA-sponsored survey of Cressida owners found reported usage rates in the 90 percent range.

The sales record of both automatic belts and air bags might have been better if dealers had presented the technologies in a more favorable light. A survey of Chevette and Rabbit owners by Opinion Research Corporation found that sales personnel tended to explain the automatic restraint system in a ''neutral'' manner. Rarely did dealers offer a positive personal opinion about the safety feature. Dealer attitudes toward air bags were no more enthusiastic.

There are several ways to interpret marketing experience with passive restraints. In public testimony, General Motors has argued that real-world marketing experience with air bags and passive belts should be viewed as reliable indicators of the absence of any significant demand for passive restraints, since they reflect actual consumer preferences in the marketplace. This conclusion is certainly arguable. Perhaps a more plausible conclusion is that marketing experience with passive restraints has been disappointing because of consumer ignorance and dealer apathy. If motorists tend to neglect their vulnerabilities to crash injury, it is no wonder that they are not anxious to pay extra for unknown safety features that are not marketed aggressively by dealers.

Dilemma of the Manufacturers

Automobile manufacturers have not been anxious to market passive restraints voluntarily and their reasons are understandable. The company that offers passive restraints must risk a loss in sales to a competitor who offers cars with familiar manual belts at a lower price. Manufacturers are extremely reluctant to offer a more expensive product than their competitors.

Disincentives to air-bag promotion are especially strong because of problems with economies of scale in production. Since there is uncertainty about the extent of consumer demand for air bags, a company would prefer to introduce the device on a low-volume basis, preferably as an option. The strategy protects the company against large losses in the event that consumers react negatively to air bags. At an optional sales volume of, say, 100,000 units, the average cost of full front-seat air-bag protection spirals to $900—1100 (1981 dollars). Few consumers would purchase air bags at this price. While air bags might generate significant consumer interest at a price of $200—300 (1981 dollars), auto makers or suppliers would have to produce over a million units per year to reduce costs below this level.

The automaker thus faces a Hobson's choice:

- make a billion-dollar commitment to air bags as standard equipment on several car lines with no assurance of customer demand or acceptance, or
- introduce air bags on a low-volume optional basis and sell the product at a loss as General Motors did from 1974—76.

In the face of this dilemma, a prudent strategy for any single company is to wait for a competitor to test the waters and then join in if sufficient consumer interest materializes. This strategy avoids substantial risk at apparently moderate costs: the air bag is not a product for which a brand name is critical to the ultimate consumer, so the first entrant may not have a lasting advantage over imitators. If all firms follow this strategy, the result is obvious: air bags are not available to consumers at any price. In fact, air bags have not been offered on any new car sold in the U.S. market since model year 1976. In a promising development, Mercedes-Benz recently announced that it will offer driver-side air bags on some of its 1984 model cars.

Competitive fears are also a deterrent to widespread installation of automatic belts. Many consumers are likely to perceive automatic belts as unsightly and obtrusive. No single manufacturer has an incentive to test how much patience consumers have for "use-enhancing" devices. Since Volkswagen Rabbit owners are more educated and safety conscious than the average new car buyer, the Volkswagen experience does not dismiss the fears of other automakers. There is certainly no evidence that Volkswagen is taking sales away from competitors because of the availability of passive belts.

From a political standpoint it may also be difficult for a company to oppose mandatory passive restraints as an onerous regulation while the devices are being marketed to customers. It is possible for the company to defend a pure free-choice position, but the corporation may want to buttress its case against regulation by making objections to the technologies. These objections are hard to maintain if the same company is advertising the devices to customers.

It is here that consumer advocates may have impaired the future of passive-restraint systems. During 1969–70 the Ford Motor Company was planning to install air bags as standard equipment on a line of full-size cars to test effectiveness and acceptance by consumers. Before the program was underway, the federal government issued a proposed rule requiring the installation of air bags in all new cars. Believing that the mandate was premature, Ford abandoned its demonstration program and joined the "anti-air bag war in Washington." A similar point is made by representatives of the dying air bag industry. A former executive of Eaton Corporation insists that if NHTSA had not attempted to mandate passive restraints in the early 1970s, air bags would be available in the market today. Safety advocates may have overplayed the regulatory game by triggering an industry backlash against the lifesaving technology.

II. PUBLIC POLICY DIRECTIONS

It is politically sensitive for government to adopt policies aimed at overcoming, correcting, or bypassing alleged deficiencies in the personal decision-making of citizens. The occupant-restraint issue, unlike many other risk-management problems, is not fundamentally a problem of risks imposed on citizens by new technologies. Although nuclear power and occupant restraints are both public-health issues, the nature of the risks are politically distinct because the injury risks of belt nonuse are perceived to be incurred voluntarily by citizens.

When government attempts to influence or regulate self-hazardous behavior, it acts with an ever-present danger of public rejection and backlash. This tendency of democracy is a healthy one because it protects our populace from the "slippery slope" of government domination. At the same time, government has a responsibility to maintain and enhance the health and general welfare of the citizenry. This is also a sensible obligation since government will frequently be in a better position than citizens to identify and initiate health-promotion activities. The tension between free choice and health protection should be given substantial weight in policy formulation. Public institutions can suffer irreparable harm by attempting to impose safety when people don't know they need or want it.

Some Unacceptable Alternatives

Over 30 countries have adopted laws that require motorists to wear safety belts. Many of these countries have succeeded in raising observed usage rates above 50 percent and several countries (notably Australia) have sustained usage rates in the 70−80 percent range. Countries with weak or nonexistent enforcement efforts (e.g., Japan and Puerto Rico) have not raised the rate of belt use significantly.

As a result of federal funding incentives, most states in the United States considered belt-use laws in the mid-1970s. Over 100 bills were introduced in 44 states, but none of the proposals were enacted into law. Although many states are now passing or considering child-restraint usage laws, little interest can be found among state legislators for an adult-restraint law.

A compulsory belt-use law is perceived as an infringement on the freedom and privacy of motorists. In most public opinion surveys, a majority of respondents oppose adoption of such a law. The widespread movement to weaken or repeal motorcycle helmet-use laws reflects, in part, a belief that paternalistic safety policies are incompatible with American values.

Safety advocates have also been pushing for a mandatory passive-restraint standard for almost 15 years. The insurance industry is now leading the fight in the Supreme Court to block the Reagan Administration's attempt to repeal the Carter Administration's passive-restraint standard. The contested passive-restraint standard, if upheld in court, will also face challenges in Congress. Even if the standard takes effect, companies will probably comply with passive belts that are easily detached by motorists. The benefits of detachable passive belts would be very modest, though still in excess of marginal costs (Graham and Gorham, 1983). Moreover, any standard would not take effect until model year 1986 or possibly several years later. Another decade must be alloted for cars with passive restraints to filter into the vehicle fleet. Teenagers, perhaps the group in most need of protection, will be the last to benefit since they rely primarily on the used-car market.

In any event, mandatory passive restraints may be unacceptable to the public. The sad reality is that it only takes a vocal minority of citizens to weaken or repeal national policies with substantial lifesaving potential. Among ideological conservatives and opponents of "Big Brother" government, opposition to nondetachable belts or air bags is likely. The opposition will be magnified since most Americans know little about passive restraints. Some people will fear being trapped in a car by automatic belts (despite the presence of emergency release mechanisms). In the case of air bags, people harbor unsubstantiated suspicions about air-bag performance and myths about air-bag hazards are perpetuated by ill-informed media stories.

Even a small probability of vocal opposition to passive restraints should be given serious consideration by policymakers. Public opposition to regulation can cause more damage than repeal of the initial regulation. It can also cause Congress to create obstacles to passage of new safety programs. For example, negative reaction to the starter interlock device in 1974 caused Congress to add a legislative-veto amendment to NHTSA's statutory authority to adopt passive restraints. Ever since the interlock fiasco, Congress has been embroiled in the passive-restraint controversy. Since a mandate of air bags and/or nondetachable belts could cause negative public reaction, it seems worthwhile to explore nonregulatory alternatives that would save lives and avoid vocal opposition.

Information to Motorists

If we postulate a continuum of policy options involving increasing amounts of government coercion of individuals, government programs to ensure that accurate information is made available are quite close to the least coercive end of the continuum. Their purpose is to facilitate individual choice by overcoming imperfections in the market for information. Over the past 15 years a variety of mass media campaigns have been attempted to promote the use of safety belts. The results were not very encouraging. For example, the National Safety Council consumed the equivalent of $51.8 million in media time and space in 1968−69 with no effect on reported usage rates. In 1970 a television advertisement was devised by the Insurance Institute for Highway Safety to promote belt use. The commercial used an appeal to friends people might have who were injured in a car crash. Despite a prime-time television campaign that would have cost $7 million if aired on a national basis, the commercial had no effect on observed usage rates in the "treatment" community.

Many foreign countries have adopted belt-use laws because they were unsuccessful in raising usage levels through promotional campaigns. Those campaigns that have a positive effect on observed usage may not necessarily change the rate of belt use *in crashes*. Even if belt use can be increased with information, it may be difficult to sustain high usage rates in the long run.

The failure of previous media campaigns should not be considered the final word on the subject of information and education. One can question whether past campaigns were done as effectively as possible. It is not obvious that the messages were optimally designed or dessiminated. A mass media campaign in Great Britain made some progress: Usage rates increased from 12 percent in 1971 to 30 percent in 1974. Reinforcement campaigns have sustained the voluntary usage rate at about 30 percent since 1974, but Great Britain has recently resorted to a compulsory belt-use law.

One new message that should be tried is the concept of lifetime risk. The probabilities of crash injury are extremely small when viewed from a "trip perspective," but are larger and easier to comprehend when aggregated over a lifetime. For example, the average driver's chances of being killed or seriously injured on a per trip basis are 26 in ten million (0.0000026 per trip). Yet over a lifetime of driving, the chances are one in seven (0.14). Two pilot projects with information campaigns have shown that the lifetime risk message can induce people to buckle their safety belts more frequently (Slovic, et al., 1978; Schwalm and Slovic, 1982).

NHTSA has recently initiated a nationwide safety belt education campaign. The goals of the program are to: (1) increase public awareness of accident risks; (2) increase public awareness of the benefits of belt use; and (3) provide information and assistance concerning specific actions individuals and organizations can take to encourage belt use. During fiscal years 1982–84, about $10 million in federal funds may be expended on the campaign.

The NHTSA campaign should be carefully evaluated to determine the effect on belt use. If usage rates do not increase, the project may still have benefits. Education can increase public awareness of accidents and create more sympathetic attitudes toward safety programs. In several foreign countries, public information and education paved the way for passage of belt-use laws. A similar effect was observed in several Michigan communities exposed to a belt-use media campaign. The percentage of motorists opposed to a mandatory belt-use law dropped from 52 to 38 percent during the campaign. For this reason the NHTSA campaign can be viewed as necessary groundwork for more aggressive occupant-restraint policies—an investment that will yield reduced hostility towards social control of auto accident risks.

The NHTSA program should be expanded to include information on passive-restraint devices. A major barrier to a passive restraint standard is public ignorance and misunderstanding of the technologies. NHTSA should use electronic and print media to disseminate photographs of how passive restraints perform in crash tests. Motorists should be provided simple statistical comparisons of how the probability of serious injury is reduced by restraint systems. The early General Motors air-bag advertisements provide an excellent introduction to the technology and Volkswagen has found that passive-belt advertisements have very high consumer retention scores compared to other automotive ads. A passive-restraint education program is essential to an effective passive-restraint policy. Such a campaign could minimize the amount of adverse public reaction to introduction of air bags and automatic belts. The campaign may also reduce the reluctance of auto manufacturers to offer passive restraints voluntarily on some new car lines.

Incentives to Buckle Up

Surprisingly little research has been done on the use of financial incentives to encourage belt use. A variety of ideas have been proposed, but no one has suggested ways to overcome the practical difficulties. In this section both "post-crash" and "pre-crash" incentives are discussed.

A post-crash incentive would be applied to motorists based on a belt-use determination after a crash has occurred. For example, several insurance companies offer expanded medical coverage to policyholders who suffer injury while belted in a crash. One company offers twice the medical payment limitation to motorists who were injured in a crash and were wearing safety belts.

Disincentives to not wearing safety belts can also be applied on a post-crash basis. In West Germany the courts reduce damage claims by 30–60 percent to those who are injured in a crash with belts unfastened. The policy is the only penalty for violation of the nation's compulsory belt-use law (i.e., fines are not issued by police).

Some courts in the United States have dealt with the issue of nonuse of safety belts in liability cases. In one case the New York Court of Appeals ruled that failure to buckle up is a factor that juries can consider in determining whether the accident victim exercised due care to avoid or lessen the severity of injury. Recovery was limited to damages for injuries that would have occurred even if the victim had been wearing safety belts. This doctrine of "contributory negligence" has not been applied extensively in the United States since belt nonuse is normal behavior among American motorists.

There is no scientific evidence indicating that post-crash incentives are effective in changing the belt-use habits of motorists. Setting aside the problem of verifying belt use, there is reason to believe that post-crash incentives would not be an effective use-promoting strategy. A major psychological barrier to belt use is the belief that the probability of a serious accident is too low to be of concern. If people discount their vulnerabilities to crash injury, then it is unlikely that marginal changes in the financial costs of an accident will change behavior. One can argue also that the adverse consequences of a crash are already so serious that it is inappropriate to further penalize crash victims and their families.

The incentive approach might be more effective if it was applied on a pre-crash basis. For example, insurance companies could offer premium discounts to policyholders who regularly wear safety belts. This arrangement creates a guaranteed financial benefit to buckling up and, therefore, bypasses the cognitive difficulties with assessing low probabilities.

Verification of belt use has (to date) been an insurmontable barrier to introduction of insurance discounts for professed belt users. Companies have no reliable basis upon which to distinguish belt users from nonusers. Observed usage rates in cars with automatic belts are two to four times higher than for comparable cars with manual belts. Nonetheless, most insurance companies say there is insufficient evidence to justify lower premiums for cars with automatic belts.

A major advance in automotive safety would be the design of a device that could monitor the belt-use behavior of motorists. A promising possibility is application of microprocessing technology. Small computers could be installed in cars that would log how many miles were traveled with belts fastened and unfastened. Separate logs could be kept for the different seating positions. With the consent of car owners, evidence from these computers could be used by insurance companies as a basis for providing differential premiums to motorists. The device would need to be relatively tamper proof and belt systems should be designed so that it is uncomfortable for a motorist to travel with the belt fastened behind the body. This is an idea that merits some attention by safety engineers.

In the immediate future other types of pre-crash incentives should be implemented, at least on an experimental basis. NHTSA is investigating the use of lotteries and prizes to promote belt use. An experiment with contingent rewards for belt use at Virginia Polytechnic Institute found that small financial rewards caused belt use among students and staff to rise from 26 percent during the baseline period to 36 percent during the ''prize'' period and to 38 percent during a short follow-up period. Similar results have been achieved in a program at the University of North Carolina.

The results from the incentive projects should be greeted with some skepticism. Do higher usage rates persist after rewards have been removed for a sustained period of time? How much would it cost to implement reward programs on a national scale so that usage rates are increased to, say, just 30−40 percent? These questions need further study. Even if these questions are not answered favorably, the reward projects have established an important fact. Many people can be induced to buckle up with small financial incentives. The most promising way to implement a financial incentive on a national scale would be through the mechanism of insurance premiums.

Modified Legal Strategies

In the mid-1970s federal funding incentives were available to states that adopted belt-use laws. Although no state adopted a law, some states came very close. At least one house in six different stage legislatures passed the law more than once. However, the 1974 NHTSA Appropriations Act contained no funding for safety belt law incentives. A survey of state officials by the American Safety Belt Council found that the chances of adopting a belt-use law are increased greatly by federal funding incentives.

The first order of business in the direction of a belt-use law should be reinstatement of federal funding incentives. This action alone is not sufficient to make belt-use laws politically tolerable. The incentive provision should be designed so that states can experiment with some modified legal strategies.

First, states should receive incentive monies for adopting laws that apply only to certain roads. For example, motorists might be more willing to accept a belt-use requirement on turnpikes, toll roads and interstates where the length of trips is usually long. It would be relatively easy to post signs at entrances to these roads reminding motorists to buckle up. These roads tend to be monitored fairly well by police so a built-in enforcement effort is already in place. If laws on these roads were received well, the concept could be applied to other roads.

Second, states should receive incentive grants if laws are passed that cover only young drivers. Making the law apply only to drivers under the age of 21 or 18 is a possibility. This segment of the driving population is involved in a disproportionate share of fatal accidents. Some states that have weakened motorcycle helmet laws have preserved the requirements for young cyclists. The case for paternalism is certainly stronger for teenagers who are inexperienced drivers with a tendency to neglect safety matters. Some states might be willing to pass teenage-restraint laws in conjunction with child-restraint laws (if federal incentives were available).

Third, states should have an incentive to consider a ''voluntary'' belt-use law. Each adult driver could define his or her own legal status with regard to belt use during the annual vehicle registration process. Drivers who promise to wear safety belts would have licensing and car-registration fees waived or reduced substantially by the state transportation department. In some states these fees amount to $20−30 per year per car. Motorists who do not promise to buckle up would pay the normal registration fees. The program would cause people to make a conscious decision about their annual belt-use behavior. A direct financial incentive would be provided to drivers who promise to buckle up.

A voluntary belt-use law would be enforced in the same manner that compulsory belt-use laws are enforced. Specially-colored license plates and owners' cards could be issued so that police could readily distinguish vehicles subject to the law. Drivers would assume responsibility for the belt-use habits of all front-seat occupants. Since belt-use laws are normally enforced by police only in the process of issuing other traffic citations, the police would not be unduly burdened and motorists would not be subjected to additional road-side stops. Motorists found to be in violation of their licensing contract would be subject to a traffic fine of, say, $50. The program would also provide insurance companies with an objective basis upon which to provide premium discounts to belt users.

Finally, stage legislators might be more willing to experiment with a belt-use law if it were passed with a ''sunset'' provision. Skeptics of the law could be assured that the policy will be terminated automatically in, say, three years unless the state legislature takes positive action to continue the law. Experience in Ontario, Canada, was that the belt-use law became more popular over time. Surveys found that the percentage of citizens opposed to the law declined from about 60 percent at the time of adoption of about 30 percent two years after the law was enforced.

The major barrier is getting the first one or two states to try some kind of adult restraint law. Once this initial hurdle is passed, a domino effect in other states may ensue. In the long run federal highway funds could be tied directly to each state's belt-use rate. For each percentage point increase in a state's belt-use rate, federal funding incentives could be increased a corresponding amount. An incentive system based on performance would encourage states to experiment with innovative approaches to belt-use promotion.

Voluntary Passive Restraints

A major breakthrough toward solving the occupant-restraint problem would be adoption of a nonregulatory policy that would encourage the availability of passive restraints on a voluntary basis. A nonregulatory policy may be preferable to a passive-restraint standard because: (1) it is more likely to be politically feasible; (2) once adopted it is less likely to generate adverse public reactions; and (3) it would be more equitable to chose who currently wear manual belts. In fact, a nonregulatory policy might be a necessary precondition to a mandatory passive-restraint standard. Voluntary passive restraints would build a political constituency for the devices and reduce opposition based on misunderstanding of the technologies.

Former Secretary of the Department of Transportation (DOT) William T. Coleman devised a promising nonregulatory policy in 1976. Believing that a passive-restraint mandate was premature, Secretary Coleman called upon the automobile manufacturers to join the federal government in a demonstration program to exhibit the effecitveness of passive restraints. By the final days of the Ford Administraton in January 1977, Coleman was successful in negotiating an agreement with the major auto manufacturers. General Motors agreed to produce up to 150,000 intermediate-sized cars with full front-seat air-bag protection while Ford Motor Company agreed to produce up to 70,000 compact cars with air bags on the driver-side of the front seat. In total, up to 500,000 cars were to be equipped with passive restraints during model years 1980 and 1981. The companies promised to advertise the devices and to sell air bags at a price well below cost ($100 for full front-seat air-bag protection in 1976 dollars).

Unfortunately, the Coleman plan never book effect. In July, 1977 the Carter Administration, represented by Brock Adams (DOT Secretary) and Joan Claybrook (NHTSA Administrator), decided to mandate passive restraints on a phased-in schedule beginning model year 1982. This action terminated the obligation of the auto companies under the Coleman agreement. Adams and Claybrook were unable to persuade the automakers to proceed with the demonstration program.

Adams and Claybrook believed that the mandatory standard would cause

60 percent of cars to be equipped with air bags and 40 percent with passive belts. They did not foresee the 1979 Iranian oil crisis, the boom in small car sales, and the depression that has afflicted the auto industry. NHTSA now estimates that companies will rely almost exclusively on detachable automatic belts to comply with the passive-restraint standard, assuming it stays in effect. Automatic belts were chosen over air bags because they were less expensive than air bags and were more readily installed in small cars without further development work. Of course the Reagan Administration is now trying to repeal the entire passive-restraint standard.

As an alternative to regulation, NHTSA has announced intentions to renegotiate a Coleman-style demonstration program. The passive-restraint issue has, therefore, come back full circle to the situation faced by Coleman. There are a number of ways that NHTSA could improve upon the original Coleman plan.

First, auto makers should be eligible for tax credits to cover the cost of passive restraints. For example, manufacturers could be permitted a $300 tax credit for each car equipped with air bags and a $100 credit for each car equipped with passive belts. NHTSA should ask Congress to pass amendments to the tax code authorizing these credits. Senator John Danforth (R-Mo.) was the first legislator to propose the tax-incentive approach, and he has expressed a strong interest in making passive restrants available to the public. Manufacturers would be less reluctant to participate in a cooperative demonstration program if tax credits were available to cover the costs of installing passive restraints.

Second, the demonstration program would include substantial offerings of both nondetachable passive belts and air bags. The program is most likely to generate consumer interest and public acceptance if consumers are provided some choice between different types of restraint systems.

Third, the program should call for passive restraints to be standard equipment on several major car lines. Previous experience with optional passive restraints suggests that dealers are unlikely to promote the devices when offered only as an option. The Coleman plan would have failed if dealers and salespeople had not marketed the devices aggressively. When a safety feature is made standard equipment, a built-in incentive exists for salespeople to present the feature in a positive light.

Finally, the program should contain assurances from insurance carriers that owners of cars with passive restraints will be eligible for insurance premium discounts. A recent survey by NHTSA found that only 10–30 percent of all automobile insurance policies nationwide offer a 30 percent discount in first-party injury premiums to vehicles with automatic restraints. NHTSA estimates that a 30 percent discount amounts to about a $65 reduction in the average annual personal injury premium per insured vehicle. This discount is a crucial feature of the demonstration program because it provides consumers with a direct financial incentive to buy cars with automatic restraints. While it may be appropriate to offer a somewhat lower discount for automatic belts (because of lower usage rates), at least 10−15 percent discount would be warranted by usage rates observed in Volkswagen Rabbits.

NHTSA may have difficulty persuading automakers to participate in a demonstration program. When former Administrator Raymond Peck announced his intention to repeal the passive-restraint standard, the agency lost the most immediate form of leverage available. Since the auto makers know NHTSA is committed to deregulation, they have little incentive to negotiate in good faith. Former Secretary Coleman found that the threat of regulation was necessary to induce companies to sign the 1977 demonstration agreement. If NHTSA is serious about orchestrating a passive-restraint demonstration program, it must be prepared to propose mandatory air bags and/or nondetachable belts as an alternative. It remains to be seen whether the regulatory threat is necessary and whether NHTSA has the political power to make a mandatory standard a credible threat to the automakers.

NOTES

1. I thank Steven Garber, Max Henrion, M. Granger Morgan, and Susan Hadden for helpful suggestions.

2. This is reported in U.S. General Accounting Office, *The Effects, Benefits, and Costs of Federal Safety Standards for the Protection of Car Occupants,* Report of the Comptroller General of the United States, Washington D.C., July 1976.

Chapter 4

THE COURTS: JUDICIAL REVIEW AND RISK ASSESSMENT
Norman J. Vig

Editor's introduction.

Of all the institutions involved in the formulation and implementation of policy, the attempt to regulate technological risks has seemed to place the most unusual burden on the courts. Not only procedural irregularities, the traditional focus of judicial oversight, but also the validity of the interpretation of scientific and technical information has been brought to the bar. Vig describes very clearly several interpretations of the judicial role in risk regulation and the strains that these different interpretatons have placed on the judiciary itself. The decisions of the activist courts, which have been based on a mixture of science, economics, and politics, illustrate as well as any other events the inappropriateness of a strict two-stage model.

As with other new areas of public policy, however, an initial burst of unuasual activity has settled into a more routine policy response. Vig suggests that the court will probably now emphasize procedural review of agency standards, limiting substantive review only to the most extraordinary cases. This will reduce the strains that risk regulation has placed on the judiciary. However, a narrower role for the court may reduce the number of points in the policy process that can trigger new iterations of policy formulation; this will in turn place an additional burden on Congress and the agencies to ensure that new information, whether scientific, economic, or political, becomes the occasion for review of established risk policy.

In a society in revolt against expertise, the judge emerges as the prophet armed—armed in his ignorance of every one of the technologies that make the society run. The judge is transformed, in his own eyes as well as those of others, from the industrial idiot to the post-industrial hero and wise man.

Martin Shapiro (1979)

INTRODUCTION

Recent critics of judicial activism have not had much respect for the courts as institutions for resolving complex scientific and technical disputes over societal risks generated by new technologies. Many scholars, such as Shapiro (1979), argue that judges lack the professional training and expertise to make rational decisions. Others, such as Green (1980), assert that risk policy decisions are essentially political and that the courts have no business substituting their judgment for that of elected representatives. Still others express more pragmatic concerns over the escalating costs of litigation and the burdens imposed on administrators by the need to anticipate court review of virtually all regulatory decisions (Melnick 1980). Last but not least, some resent the broad access to the courts that citizens and interest groups have gained in the past decade, allowing them to challenge many policy decisions. As should become evident in this paper, we do not fully accept any of these arguments.

Part of the problem lies in the conventional view of risk assessment outlined by Hadden in the introductory chapter. If, as Lowrance (1976) and others claim, risk assessment is properly disaggregated into "risk measurement" (a scientific process) and "risk acceptability" (a political judgment), then the courts would seem to have very little role to play. Being neither technically expert nor politically accountable, judges are ipso facto incompetent when it comes to risk assessment. And, if they do not recognize their incompentence, courts will only undermine their own legitimacy as authoritative institutions (O'Brien, 1982).

In my opinion, this kind of reductionist logic is far too simplistic. If we could neatly disaggregate risk policy problems into "scientific" and "value" components and assign institutional responsibilities for handling each part in logical sequence, then there would be little in principle to disagree about. But the real world is vastly different as we all know. We cannot even *define* a risk problem without considering public acceptability, and as the other chapters in this book indicate, no institution operates without implicit bias in evaluating potential harm. The uncertainties present in all risk analysis cannot be wished away or delegated to any one company of experts. Whether we like it or not, social risk management requires holistic judgments which no single institution is uniquely competent to make. Moreover, we live in a litigous society in which access to the courts is itself an important democratic value. The legitimate extent and nature of judicial intervention is always an important constitutional question, but to deny judicial competency in a technologically complex society—in which many issues literally involve matters of life and death— is, to an important degree, to deny the potentials for the rule of law as most people conceive it.

Hadden's argument that risk policy decisions are characterized by high personal salience, uncertainty of information, and redistributive consequences, raises more troublesome questions about the role of the courts. She is surely right in pleading for greater recognition of the ''political'' dimensions of risk decision-making. But does it necessarily follow that the courts should play a more passive and restrained role? Given other institutional weaknesses, we do not think that it does. Although other forums are better suited to expressing public concerns, generating scientific information, and weighing distributive consequences, courts *can* provide a valuable ''second look'' which integrates these components, clarifies the bases of decision-making, and ensures reasoned application to specific circumstances. That is not to argue that they always do so, but anyone who reads the law journal literature knows that the potentials for creative judicial interpretation are there. In our present state of knowledge—or lack thereof— there is a strong case for pluralistic approaches to risk evaluation in different institutional settings.

In any case, the courts cannot avoid passing judgment on many aspects of public policy, especially when new fields of public law develop. The flood of new health, safety, consumer, and environmental laws of the 1970s forced them to review innumerable regulatory decisions. It has been a mammoth task to sort out congressional intent regarding different social risks and to identify ambiguities in the statutes. It is absurb to argue (as does Shapiro) that the courts invited litigation by posing as post-industrial guardians of consumer and other general public interests against the evils of technology run wild. Because Congress adopted vague standards and failed to resolve many important questions, the courts have been overwhelmed by litigation. Indeed, most recent statutes provide for direct review of administrative decisions in the federal appellate courts. Congress evidently *intended* the courts to play an active part in refining agency policy.

There are certainly problems in placing this heavy burden on the courts. Judicial resources have been strained to the limit, and the social costs of litigation have been high. Different groups and interests do not have equal access to the courts because of the high price of legal talent (Galanter 1974). But these inequities affect other institutional processes as well, and public interest groups and other organizations such as union legal departments have generally done a good job of defending citizens and workers against unwanted risks.

The functions, structure, and processes of the judicial system are discussed in the section which follows. I then look more closely at the role of the courts in reviewing risk policy decisions and the kinds of choices they must make. Following that, I discuss several recent cases in which the scope of judicial review has been narrowed by the Supreme Court. Finally, I offer some concluding comments on the current status of judicial review in this area.

JUDICIAL FUNCTIONS, STRUCTURE, AND PROCESS

The judicial role in assessing risks is scarcely new. For centuries Anglo-Saxon courts have recognized common law doctrines for protecting society against individual negligence and public nuisance. On occasion, they have had to draw the line on private actions which might so endanger the public health and welfare that injunction is required. Under civil tort law, courts have also had to resolve disputes among private parties over alleged injury and damage (Baram 1982). Indeed, until recently the courts were often the only recourse for those threatened by harm, but generally it was necessary to prove actual injury before injunction or compensation could be won. In other words, the judicial system largely acted *retrospectively* rather than prospectively. It was the inadequacy of the courts as a mechanism for protecting society against future risks that produced the new legislation of the 1970s. For the first time in history, a comprehensive body of public law was enacted to protect the nation against *prospective* as well as current risk.

This obviously changed the functions of the courts in risk assessment. One of their most important tasks now became one of interpreting and applying risk policy statutes, which in turn involved them in the administration of the law. Moreover, the timing of the new legislation coincided with a broader movement within the federal judiciary to exert tighter supervision over the discretionary authority of regulatory agencies (Stewart 1975). The growing delegation of informal rulemaking powers to such agencies had become increasingly troublesome to many federal judges. In early 1971, David Bazelon, then Chief Judge of the D. C. Court of Appeals, proclaimed "a new era in the history of the long and fruitful collaboration of administrative agencies and reviewing courts," in which courts would "require administrative officers to articulate the standards and principles that govern their discretionary decisions in as much detail as possible" (EDF v. Ruckelshaus, 439 F.2d 597–98).

Although this marked a turn toward greater judicial activism, it was also true that many of the new laws reflected public and congressional dissatisfaction with the practices of the older independent regulatory commissions to whose judgments the courts had largely deferred since the New Deal (Ackerman and Hassler 1981). Congress included generous provisions for citizen suits in several statutes and required judicial intervention at many points in an effort to ''open up'' government to the public. Court efforts to ensure full public disclosure of the bases for agency decision making became an important judicial function, along with substantive review of agency actions. However, the relative weight to be given to different types of procedural and substantive review was to become a divisive issue within the courts (see next section).

Courts normally have their greatest impact in the early stages of a policy cycle. When the laws are implemented and litigated for the first time, courts have to construe the intent of the legislation and the boundaries of delegated authority. In doing so, they reveal ambiguities and conflicts in the law, frequently leading to legislative revision. If Congress does not respond, the judiciary can have major impacts on policy implementation. By the same token, as the meaning of the law is clarified and administration becomes routinized, the judicial impact normally declines (although specific decisions can always be appealed). The problem in most areas of risk policy is that Congress has been reluctant or unable to clarify its own intent. This is understandable in light of the inherent complexities of risk decision-making and the need for administrative flexibility in defining standards governing a vast array of changing technologies. Nevertheless, it has prolonged the involvement of the courts and, in some cases, led them to impose standards which appear to many to violate basic statutory purpose (as in the ''benzene'' case to be discussed later). At the same time, the courts have become increasingly frustrated over their heavy burden and the lack of clear legislative guidance.

The structure of the court system adds further to the dilemma. There are more than a hundred federal district and circuit courts which often make inconsistent decisions. Although the courts of Appeal and ultimately the Suprme Court resolve some of the most important differences, judicial outputs can be as diverse in the aggregate as those of the other branches of government. This was recently illustrated, for example, in an empirical analysis of some 1900 federal environmental cases decided in the 1970s which demonstrated that plaintiffs of various kinds did considerably better at certain levels of the judicial sytem and in some circuits than in others (Wenner 1982). In the lengthy *Reserve Mining* litigation, federal and state courts at four different levels each approached questions of risk assessment differently and arrived at widely different conclusions as to the hazards of water- and air-borne asbestiform fibers (Vig 1979). Although the Court of Appeals for the District of Columbia has greatest responsibility for reviewing federal administrative decisions, its efforts at formulating new doctrines for evaluating uncertain risks have largely been frustrated by other circuits and the Supreme Court. Divisions within the D.C. Circuit and the Supreme Court have added to the confusions, as will be seen later.

Can the courts then play a more constructive role in risk decision making? In our view, the most relevant questions have to do with judicial *process*. It is often argued, even by judges, that the adversarial nature of court procedure is inappropriate for the resolution of technical controversies because it polarizes opinion rather than facilitating the search for scientific "truth" (Markey in U.S. Congress, Joint Hearings). Lawyers on each side will present the strongest possible case regardless of its scientific merit. They will selectively cite expert opinion and evidence which supports their argument, while seeking to discredit that of the adversary by whatever means are available. Judges are then left to pick and choose among conflicting scientific evidence, much of it distorted in the process. This is an exaggerated portrayal of reality (Bereano 1974), but many have concluded that special "science courts" or other mechanisms are needed to separate out and evaluate the technical issues in legal controversies (see Rushevsky, this volume). And, while the original science court proposal (Kantrowitz 1976) met with little enthusiasm in the legal community, the American Bar Association has joined scientific organizations in an effort to devise better rules for technical adjudication (Markey 1982).

I do not object to experimentation of this kind, but I doubt that it will provide viable solutions to many legal disputes involving risk assessment. It may be impossible to find mutually acceptable scientific judges, and the timing and scope of the inquiry are critically important in determining *which* technical issues are adjudicated (Casper 1976). But the greatest problem in all risk decision-making is the inherent uncertainty of information *and knowledge* (Latin 1982). Even when information is available or attainable at reasonable cost (e.g., through further research), "knowledgeable" experts will still disagree over interpretaton of data and its policy implications. These disagreements cannot help but enter into the political and legal aspects of the case so long as courts have to decide whether agency actions are reasonable in light of the statute.

The more practical question then is how regular judicial procedures affect decision making under conditions of uncertainty. There is no simple answer, because judges differ widely in their approach and have a great deal of latitude in deciding how to apply conventional legal rules. However, I would argue that conventional legal processes (like scientific methodology!) are still very much directed toward maintaining standards of proof for establishing certainty. It is true that such standards are not the same in the courtroom as in the scientific laboratory. Courts generally have to settle for a higher degree of ambiguity, accepting evidence, for example, that is "more likely than not." Nevertheless, the standard rules of procedure are relatively conservative on such matters as the admissibility of evidence and assignment of the burden of proof. For example, even when statutes allow flexible approaches to the determination of "unreasonable risk of injury," the courts may impose traditional standards which make it impossible to regulate because many variables are unknown (and "unknowable" at our present stage of knowledge). Such "reductive treatment'' of uncertainty can frustrate legislative intent (Latin 1982).

At a minimum, then, some innovation in judicial procedure and doctrine is necessary if courts are to retain their legitimacy as authoritative arbiters in such disputes. The following section looks more closely at the kinds of decisions judges have to make in construing risk policy statutes and in devising a review strategy. These choices have produced some innovations but have also divided the courts.

JUDICIAL CHOICES AND DOCTRINES

Judicial decision-making must be analyzed on at least two levels. On one level, the courts have to resolve a host of questions arising from the particular requirements of the statute itself. Current laws vary greatly in the standards, definitions, and procedures they establish for evaluating risks and relating them to other policy considerations (Doniger 1978; Ricci and Molton 1981). Few laws (like the ''Delaney Amendment'' to the Food and Drug Act) require absolute risk avoidance. Most legislation instead attempts to set reasonable goals for achievable risk frequently found in the laws: *threshold or significance tests,* which define or imply a minimal level of risk acceptability (i.e., below which the agency is not empowered to regulate); *feasibility tests,* usually requiring risk reduction to the limits of technical and/or economic feasibility (thus also setting upper limits on regulatory requirements); and *balancing tests,* usually requiring that the benefits of risk reduction be weighed against the economic costs (though not necessarily through formal cost-benefit analysis). It matters a great deal which of these requirements are—or are not—found in the law, and how clearly or forcefully they are stated. Judges must decide how stringent Congress intended regulation to be, and apply the appropriate tests to the cases at hand. Overall, they must come to a conclusion as to whether the agency decision is reasonable in light of all these considerations. The range of judicial choice on this level is suggested in Table 3.

Judges do not, however, simply respond to the particular statute and controversy at hand; they are also motivated by their own norms and doctrines. Among other things, they make ''strategic'' choices on how to approach their reviewing task, what decision-rules to follow, and how far to intervene in administrative affairs. At this second level of analysis, then, we need to consider these strategic choices and how they affect judicial roles in risk assessment.

A simple way of conceptualizing the alternatives is presented in Figure 2, which juxtaposes the most fundamental distinctions found in the conventional literature on risk assessment and on judicial review. On the horizontal axis we place the usual distinction between (technical) risk measurement and (political) risk acceptability; i.e., between ''facts'' and ''values.'' Whether such a distinction is theoretically valid or not, we

Table 3
Choices in Judicial Review of Risk Policy Statutes

I. Procedural	1. Administrative procedure	a.	Were procedures followed by agency appropriate under APA and enabling statute? Are additional procedures required by law?
		b.	Was each step in the process adequately and fairly carried out?
		c.	Has a "full administrative record" been produced?
	2. Judicial/legal procedure	a.	Has the issue been appropriately raised in court?
		b.	What is the appropriate standard of judicial review ("standard of proof")?
		c.	Where does the burden of proof lie?
II.	3. Threshold tests	a.	Does agency have statutory authority to regulate the risk?
		b.	Is there sufficient evidence of risk to permit specific regulation (minimum significance threshold)?
Decision Criteria	4. Feasibility tests	a.	Must action meet test of "technical feasibility?" (i) what degree of feasibility or technology is required (e.g. "best available technology")? (ii) is proposed standard or action feasible?
		b.	Must action meet test of "economic feasibility?" (i) what factors must be considered in determining economic feasibility? (ii) is proposed standard or action feasible?
		c.	Must action meet both feasibility tests simultaneously?
	5. Balancing tests	a.	Is formal cost/benefit or risk/benefit analysis required? (i) must estimates be quantified? (ii) must estimated benefits exceed (or bear some "reasonable" relationship to) estimated costs?
		b.	How are quantified and unquantified factors to be weighted?
		c.	How are these factors to be related to other policy considerations under the statute?
III. Resolution	6. Rationality tests	a.	Is action based on "substantial evidence" (or test defined in 2b.)?
		b.	How are uncertainties to be resolved? (i) seek additional information (e.g., more research)? (ii) statutory interpretation (e.g., does statute imply error on the side of safety)?
		c.	Is the overall decision "reasonable?" (i) is action proper exercise of agency discretion under law? (ii) have all relevant factors been adequately considered and balanced?
	7. Disposition	a.	Approval (in part or entirety)
		b.	Disapproval (in part or entirety) (i) remand to agency (ii) finding of unconstitutionality (iii) finding of ultra vires

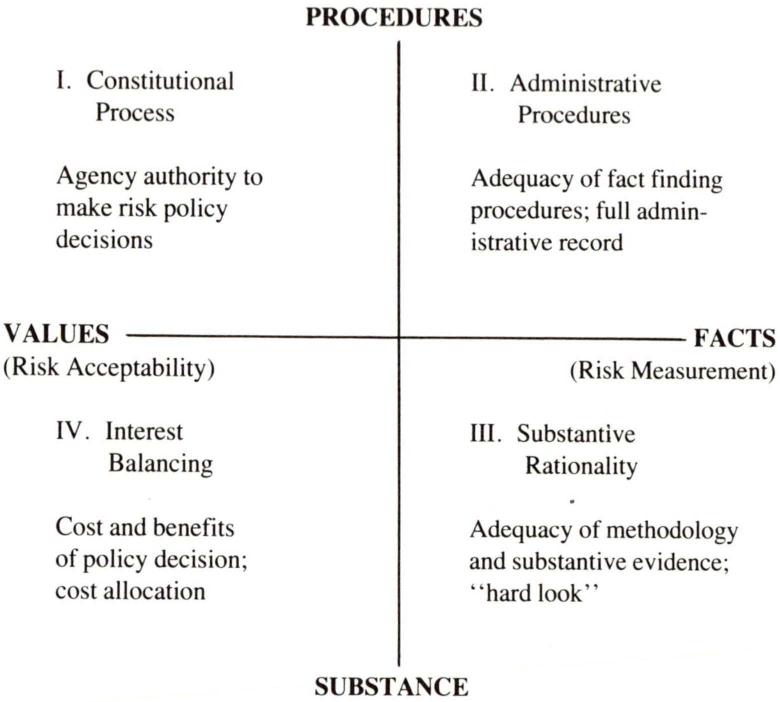

PROCEDURES

I. Constitutional
    Process

Agency authority to
make risk policy
decisions

II. Administrative
     Procedures

Adequacy of fact finding
procedures; full admin-
istrative record

VALUES ——————————————— **FACTS**
(Risk Acceptability)   (Risk Measurement)

IV. Interest
     Balancing

Cost and benefits
of policy decision;
cost allocation

III. Substantive
      Rationality

Adequacy of methodology
and substantive evidence;
"hard look"

SUBSTANCE

Figure 2. Types of Judicial Review

hypothesize that in approaching risk policy review, judges decide whether to evaluate the technical bases for the agency's risk estimation or to concentrate their review on the value choices made by the agency (in light of risk-acceptability criteria in the statute or the constitutional authority of the agency to make such policy judgments). On the vertical axis we place the traditional legal distincton between procedural and substantive review. We hypothesize that judges decide whether to focus on the processes by which authority is delegated and exercised (procedural questions) or on the substantive merit of the evidence or the policy outcome. Combining these variables in one matrix, we get four cells representing alternative modes of review.

In type I review, the court focuses on whether the agency has properly exercised authority in making decisions on risk acceptability. This normally involves questions of statutory interpretation: whether the agency's action conforms to the language and intent of the law, including criteria such as those listed in Table 3. However, it may also involve deeper constitutional issues, such as whether Congress has improperly delegated legislative powers to the agency by failing to clarify statutory purposes (e.g., the degree of safety to be accorded to the public, or criteria for balancing other policy considerations). In some cases, notably the recent decisions on OSHA regulation of benzene and cotton dust, certain Supreme Court justices have revived the delegation doctrine in an effort to strike down risk policy statutes as unconstitutionally vague. More typically, it boils down to a question of how much deference the court is willing to pay to agency discretion. There is nothing new about this type of review.

In type II review, the court directs its attention to the administrative procedures followed by the agency in reaching its decision. Procedural review is also traditional, but it took on much greater intensity and significance in the 1970s as Judge Bazelon and others attempted to make it a tool for administrative reform by forcing agencies to document the full reasoning behind their decisions. Although the Administrative Procedure Act (APA) and other general statutes such as the National Environmental Policy Act (NEPA) establish broad procedural standards for federal agencies, many risk policy laws required or implied additional fact-finding procedures (special hearings, scientific consultation, etc.). Some courts thus began to scrutinize agency procedures in much greater detail to ensure that hearings had been fairly and adequately conducted, that all relevant evidence had been considered, and that a full administrative record had been compiled. However, this approach stopped short of judicial evaluation of substantive technical findings or conclusions (e.g., the scientific validity of risk measurements).

In type III review, the court goes further and examines the underlying scientific and technical evidence, including the methodologies and conclusions of the experts involved. The issue becomes one of substantive rationality: whether the agency's decision is adequately supported by scientific and technical evidence on risk potentials. This approach requires judges to resolve questions of scientific uncertainty—at least in their own minds—and thus presents both the greatest opportunities and the greatest pitfalls for "deep" judicial inquiry. In the 1970s, some federal judges who were sensitive to the problems inherent in risk measurement advocated this approach under the rubric of the judicial "hard look" (see below). But other judges, including some members of the Supreme Court, have also not hesitated to discredit agency decisions on their scientific merit regardless of the inherent difficulties of establishing proof.

The focus in type IV review is not on procedural issues or on the technical rationality of risk estimates, but rather on the balance to be struck between conflicting interests and values. Courts have always sought to balance equities and conveniences in determining remedies at civil law, but in risk policy cases they usually seek to define acceptable levels of risk which minimize economic costs and burdens to the regulated parties. Whether the statute requires or allows such balancing is of course an important consideraton; but when the law is ambiguous, judges following this approach will frequently read some kind of cost-benefit logic into congressional intent or impose their own cost-benefit criteria. Some courts have required formal cost-benefit justification, while others have framed their judgments in terms of economic "feasibility" criteria. Since such decisions have direct distributive consequences, they also raise questions about judicial competence (to what extent should courts make decisions on cost internalizaton).

Of course, the particular case brought by plaintiffs may channel review in one direction or another. Moreover, the different review strategies are not mutually exclusive, and are sometimes combined in a single judicial opinion. Yet judges tend to prefer one strategy over another since each implies a different conception of judicial competence and the appropriate role of the court. Differences of this kind gave rise to spirited and sometimes acrimonious debates within the higher federal judiciary and among legal commentators in the 1970s as various judges and courts attempted to articulate doctrinal principles in support of review strategies. For much of the decade, attention centered around efforts of "activist" judges to establish new principles for type II and type III review involving deep judicial scrutiny of the procedures and techniques for risk measurement. Doctrinal innovations emanating from the circuit courts were at the heart of this controversy, but the Supreme Court itself was responsible for much of the confusion.

Shortly after Judge Bazelon pronounced a "new era" in the relationships between administrative agencies and reviewing courts, the Supreme Court appeared to legitimate the new judicial activism in its landmark decision in *Citizens to Preserve Overton Park, Inc.* v. *Volpe* (1971). The opinion held that agencies must base their decisions on a "full administrative record'' and that courts should conduct a ''thorough, probing, in-depth review of the facts and make a ''substantial inquiry'' to determine ''whether the decision was based on a consideration of the relevant factors and whether there has been a clear error of judgment'' (401 U.S. 415−16). This implied careful judicial scrutiny of both procedural adequacy and the substantive rationality of agency decisions. The D.C. Circuit took it to support a ''searching inquiry'' into both aspects of decision-making, but judges differed over whether to emphasize procedural (type II) or substantive (type III) factors. Bazelon argued strenuously (Bazelon 1979) for stringent procedural review to ensure that agencies had fully ''ventilated'' the issues in public hearings and given reasoned consideration to all relevant factors. Meanwhile, his colleage on the D.C. bench, Judge Harold Leventhal, had articulated the need of a judicial ''hard look'' at the substantive as well as the procedural bases for decisions ''on the frontiers of scientific knowledge'' (Leventhal 1974).

In a number of opinions, such as *Internatonal Harvester Co.* v. *Ruckelshaus* (478 F.2d 615, 1973) and *Ethyl Corp.* v. *EPA* (541 F.2d 1, 1976), Bazelon chastised his colleagues for delving too deeply into technical issues beyond the understanding of judges (for commentary see Drechsler 1977). In the pathbreaking *Ethyl* decision, in which Judge J. Skelly Wright wrote for the D.C. Court in upholding EPA regulation of lead additives in gasoline in the absence of certain scientific evidence, Bazelon went so far as to warn that ''substantive review of mathematical and scientific evidence by technically illiterate judges is dangerously unreliable'' (quoted in Oakes 1977, 498). His main concern was that the courts ''establish a *decision-making process* [within agencies] which assures a reasoned decision that can be held up to the scrutiny of the scientific community and the public'' (Bazelon 1979 [emphasis added]). This approach, though more limited in scope than that of the ''hard look,'' nevertheless resulted in frequent demands to administrative agencies suggesting fact-finding procedures beyond those required by the APA and, in some cases, beyond those specifically mandated by the controlling regulatory statute (Scalia 1979). When Bazelon's court invalidated the Nuclear Regulatory Commission's licensing procedures in the *Vermont Yankee* case (below), the Supreme Court unanimously rejected this approach to judicial review.

The ''hard look'' doctrine has been invoked in numerous cases to justify detailed judicial examination of policy premises, including methodologies utilized in risk assessment. According to Rodgers (1979, 705−706).

> Courts taking a hard look must become sufficiently acquainted with technical matters in the record to understand why the agency did what it did. The administrator through the record must be in a position to explain to the court ''the reasons why he

> chooses to follow one course rather than another.'' Under the
> doctrine assumptions must be spelled out, inconsistenciesexp-
> lained, methodologies disclosed, contradictory evidence rebut-
> ted, record references solidly grounded, guesswork eliminated
> and conclusions supported in a ''manner capable of judicial
> understanding'' [references ommitted.]

In other words, judges must be convinced of the technical rationality of the decision and pass judgment on the agency's conclusions in light of its assumptions, methodologies, and evidence. Although this presumes that lay judges have enough technical sophistication to evaluate conflicting (but fully ''explained'') arguments, it obviously does not imply complete understanding of the ''science'' involved (few public decision-makers would meet this criterion). Litigating parties recognize these limitations, but often prefer this approach as it focuses attention on their attempts to rebut the scientific claims on the other side. Agencies may resent it but find it less obtrusive than detailed supervision of their administrative proce- dures (as in Type II review). The courts themselves may find it impossible to avoid considering the underlying technical evidence in deciding whether the final agency action is ''reasonable.''

Although the ''hard look'' doctrine was initially supported by judges who were concerned that agencies were not giving sufficient attention to new scientific evidence regarding health and safety hazards, in practice it cuts both ways as it can be used to discredit uncertain evidence on these matters. Courts can, as in the *Ethyl* and *Reserve Mining* cases, use it to permit regulation of highly uncertain risks (Brown 1976; Drechler 1977). On the other hand, judges who want ''guesswork eliminated'' can demand rigorous standards of proof before regulation is upheld. Much of the controversy thus comes down to how judges interpret and apply rules pertaining to evidence and burden of proof. As suggested in the previous section, conventional rules of judicial process may inhibit constructive treatment of uncertain risks at this point.

The situation is further complicated by the fact that administrative rules of procedure are themselves in flux. For example, the traditional distinc- tion in the APA between ''formal'' and ''informal'' rule making has largely broken down as new regulatory laws have established numerous separate requirements and ''hybrid'' procedures (Stewart 1978). This has blurred any difference between the old ''substantial evidence'' test for formal adjudication and ''arbitrary and capricious'' test for informal rule-making, often requiring judicial imagination to define *some* standard of review. Although the great majority of agency decisions are now made under relatively informal proceedings, Congress may nevertheless require ''substantial evidence'' or some other standard of proof (which is rarely clear). Another complication in recent years is the flood of executive orders requiring additional cost-benefit, cost-effectiveness, and other regulatory impact analysis within agencies—often with little guidance on use of the methodologies involved (Kraft, this volume). To what extent should the courts consider the integrity of these processes in evaluating risk-benefit decisions? In short, the courts are left with large areas of discretion when they attempt to take a "hard look" at the agencies' reasoning.

The alternative, of course, is a more restricted (but not necessarily less "active") judicial role which leaves all scientific and technical judgments to the agencies and focuses on statutory and constitutional interpretation or interest balancing (types I and IV review). These approaches might be a catalyst for forcing Congress to clarify its policy intent, and certainly raise fewer questions about the technical competence of the courts (if not the Congress). For those concerned about health and safety risks, however, recent trends in this direction do not necessarily bode well. Restriction of legislative delegation could undermine entire regulatory programs, while, on the other hand, uncritical deference to agency discretion would allow increasingly "political" manipulation of the law (as we have seen, for example, in the Environmental Protection Agency). From this perspective, type IV review can be equally dangerous as it shifts attention from basic statutory intent (prevention of unacceptable risks) to *acceptable means* (efforts to minimize regulatory burdens).

DIVISIONS IN THE SUPREME COURT

Although the Supreme Court has not ruled definitively on the proper role of courts in assessing risks of future harm, recent decisions suggest that the majority of justices are seeking to restrict judicial functions after a decade of activism. However, the record remains somewhat mixed, indicating differences of approach which are not fully resolved. In one series of cases, beginning with *Vermont Yankee Nuclear Power Corp.* v. *NRDC* (1978), the court has severely restricted type II procedural review and come down hard on the side of deference to agency expertise "at the frontiers of science." In contrast, the court did not hesitate to evaluate "significant risk" in a split decision in *Industrial Union Department* v. *American Petroleum Institute (1980), the benzene case. If there is a common thread, it is that the highest* court will only insist that regulatory agencies meet what the judges perceive as statutory minima in establishing risk significance. While agencies must still take a "hard look" at the facts in the record before issuing rules, the courts are no longer authorized to engage in the kind of "deep" judicial scrutiny implied by types II and III review.

Litigation in the nuclear power plant cases began in 1974 when the Atomic Energy Commission (later Nuclear Regulatory Commission) proposed a rule that excluded nuclear waste storage and disposal from consideraton under the National Environmental Policy Act in granting individual

power plant licenses. On appeal, the D.C. Circuit Court found the procedures followed by the Commision in its generic assessment of the risks
associated with the spent fuel cycle to be grossly deficient, especially as
regards the Commission's assumption that eventual deep disposal of high-
level radioactive wastes would produce ''zero release'' into the environment
(*Natural Resources Defense Council* v. *NRC*, 547 F.2d 633, 1976). Judge
Bazelon, noting the uncertainties involved, argued that ''this type of agency
action cannot pass muster as reasoned decision-making'' (see Bazelon
1979), and the D.C. Court remanded the case to the NRC with suggestions
for further fact-finding procedures to fully ''ventilate'' the issues of waste
disposal. But on further appeal, the Supreme Court issued a scathing (and
unanimous) reversal of the circuit court (*Vermont Yankee Nuclear Power
Corp.* v. *NRDC*, 435 U.S. 519). Justice Rehnquist's opinion accused the
lower court of attempting to legislate energy policy and contained the
following blanket injunction:

> [N]othing in the APA, NEPA, the circumstances of this case, the
> nature of the issues being considered, past agency practice, or the
> statutory mandate under which the Commission operates permit-
> ted the court to review and overturn the rulemaking proceeding of
> the basis of the procedural devices employed (or not employed)
> by the Commission so long as the Commission employed at least
> the statutory *minima* [435 U.S. 548].

The Supreme Court remanded the decision for review under the standard
APA ''arbitrary and capricious'' test, making it clear that the courts had no
power to impose additional ''hybrid'' procedures on the agencies. Bazelon's
type II strategy was thus implicitly rejected.

   The National Resources Defense Council (NRDC) and the State of New
York subsequently petitioned for review of the final NRC rule issued in 1979
which retained the ''zero-release'' assumption even though the Commission
acknowledged that this assumption was ''surrounded with uncertainty.''
The D.C. Court of Appeals again upheld the challenge, this time on grounds
that exclusion of all uncertainties concerning disposal technology from the
licensing of future plants was arbitrary and capricious and did not meet the
requirements of NEPA (685 F. 2d 459). But on June 6, 1983, the
Supreme Court unanimously reversed again, holding that the NRC had
adequately disclosed and considered the uncertainties in reaching its conclusion that the probabilities of environmental contamination were insignificant
(*Baltimore Gas & Electric Co.* v. *NRDC*, No. 82-524). In her opinion,
Justice Sandra Day O'Connor expressed what has apparently come to be the
dominant view of the court:

[A] reviewing court must remember that the Commission is making predictions, within its area of special expertise, at the frontiers of science. When examining this kind of scientific determination, as opposed to simple findings of fact, a reviewing court must generally be at its most deferential [slip opinion, 16].

Other dicta indicated further that the court is no longer willing to probe very deeply into the procedural and substantive actions of agencies so long as they "articulate" the grounds for their decisions:

It is not our task to determine what decision we, as Commissioners, would have reached. Our only task is to determine whether the Commission has considered the relevant factors and articulated a rational connection between the facts found and the choice made [slip opinion, 18].

While these statements are sufficiently ambiguous to permit detailed review in special circumstances, they clearly suggest reversion to more traditional standards of review.

This decision stands in stark contrast to the Supreme Court's ruling in the benzene case three years earlier. In that case the court affirmed a decision of the Fifth Circuit Court in New Orleans which invalidated a new Occupational Safety and Health Administration standard that would have lowered the permissable level of worker exposure to benzene (a known cause of leukemia and other diseases) from 10 ppm to 1 ppm. The circuit court struck down the standard on two grounds: (1) that OSHA had not demonstrated a "significant" risk to health at existing exposure levels; (2) that the agency had failed to show a "reasonable relationship" between estimated costs and benefits before issuing the new standard. In effect, the New Orleans court read "threshold" and "balancing" tests into the law and exercised type III and IV review (in evaluating evidence on health risks and imposing cost-benefit criteria). The Supreme Court upheld the threshold significance test in *Industrial Union Department* v. *American Petroleum Institute* (448 U.S. 607) by a 5 to 4 decision supported by no less than four separate concurring opinions.

The "plurality" opinion of Justice Stevens upheld the lower court's finding that OSHA had failed to prove a significant health risk to workers at the current (10 ppm) limit, largely accepting industry claims that no adverse effects had been demonstrated at this level. OSHA's contention that no meaningful dose-response curve could be calculated from existing data at this level and that no "safe" exposure threshold could therefore be established, was rejected on grounds that the agency had not fully considered epidemiological evidence, and, in any event, bore the responsibility of *quantitatively* estimating the risks. Although Stevens stated that this requirement need not be considered a "mathematical straight-jacket" forcing the agency to "calculate the exact probability of harm," he was exceedingly unclear as to what degree of quantification might suffice. At another point, for example, he asserted that "substantial evidence" need not consist of "anything approaching scientific certainty," and that some risks are "plainly acceptable and others are plainly unacceptable." In a brief concurring opinion, Chief Justice Burger admitted that this standard of proof was ambiguous, but endorsed the general opinion that some risks are plainly necessary:

"plainly acceptable and others are plainly unacceptable." In a brief concurring opinion, Chief Justice Burger admitted that this standard of proof was ambiguous, but endorsed the general opinion that some risks are plainly necessary:

> When the administration record reveals only scant or minimal risk of material health impairment, responsible administration calls for avoidance of extravagant, comprehensive regulation. Perfect safety is a chimera: regulation must not strangle human activity in search of the impossible [448 U.S. 664].

He obviously equated uncertain evidence with "scant or minimal risk." In still another opinion, Justice Powell recognized that quantitative risk estimation might not be feasible, but that in this circumstance the agency must provide substantial evidence both for this finding and for any "qualitative" judgment regarding risks—tests which he claimed OSHA failed to meet. Powell would also have required OSHA to meet a cost-benefit balancing test, whereas the plurality left this question undecided. Finally, Justice Rehnquist concurred solely on grounds that the statute was impermissably ambiguous, amounting to an unconstitutional delegation of legislative authority (Scalia 1980).

Aside from the manifest confusion, what stands out in these opinions is (1) that the court was willing to read a threshold or significance test into a law where none explicitly exists; (2) that the court followed standard APA procedures in assigning the full burden of proof to the rulemaking agency (see Latin 1982); (3) that the court imposed a requirement for quantitative proof which the agency found impossible to meet; and (4) that the court was willing to pass judgment on the relevance and quality of the scientific evidence, uncertain as it was. Put bluntly, the court was not willing in this instance to permit regulation of an uncertain risk despite the plain language in the statute calling for protection "to the extent feasible." The tortured construction of the plurality allowed it to engage in type III review of substantive technical evidence, but without any "hard look" at the particular difficulties of establishing proof at low exposure levels. Dicta by Burger and Powell also indicted proclivities toward type IV balancing without concern for the hierarchy of values embodied in the law. [1]

On the other hand, Justice Marshall issued a blistering dissent (joined by three others) upholding the discretionary authority of OSHA and attacking the plurality for meddling in scientific judgments beyond the understanding of the court. Noting the highly protective language of the statute, he argued that the court had no business second-guessing the agency experts on questions of uncertainty. In retrospect, it is this point of view that has come to prevail in the Supreme Court since the frightful divisions in *Industrial Union*. Marshall's dissent is echoed clearly in Justice O'Connor's opinion in *Baltimore Gas & Electric*.[2] But it remains to be seen if the court will accord the same degree of deference to OSHA and other agencies as it has now given to the Nuclear Regulatory Commission.[3]

CONCLUSION

We agree with David O'Brien that, ''Contrary to critics of regulatory agencies and advocates of reliance on the marketplace and judicially enforced property rights, the judiciary seems an inauspicious forum for public policy formulation'' (O'Brien 1982, 101). Congress, and not the courts, should make fundamental decisions on risk acceptability and allocation of the costs and burdens. The courts must exercise restraint in conducting what we called type I and IV review lest they usurp these basic policy functions. But Congress cannot legislate precisely on optimal procedures and techniques for risk measurement or foresee all possible hazards. This means that the agencies require substantial discretion in setting standards and enforcing rules. However, our system also demands judicial review to prevent discretionary abuse, and the courts have a necessary role in ensuring the integrity of risk evaluation processes and methodologies. Judicial abdication is not the answer (Goldsmith and Banks 1983).

Recent judicial decisions suggest that, true to policy cycle theory, the role of the courts is contracting as risk decision-making becomes an established policy function. The Supreme Court has gradually closed the door on ''activist'' type II and III review over the past five years, while leaving it enough ajar to take a ''hard look'' at agency discretion if circumstances seem to warrant it. This may serve as a viable compromise strategy, given the difficulties courts have had in evaluating uncertain scientific evidence in the context of a bewildering variety of statutory provisions and changing administrative procedures. But uncritical deference to the agencies carries its own dangers, especially given recent conservative trends in administration. It is a truism that the courts bend with the political winds, and the present Supreme Court is no exception. Should Judge Bazelon's ''new partnership'' now take the form of an increasingly conservative agency – court alliance, current risk policy could be seriously undermined.

Vacuous statements such as Chief Justice Burger's that ''perfect safety is a chimera'' detract from the prestige and integrity of the court. Congress never intended to eliminate *all* risks. But the hard fact is that quantitative methods of risk assessment comprise a highly imperfect ''science'' and remain an inadequate basis for health and safety decision making. It is thus doubtful that present efforts to enhance the role of technical experts in agency policymaking or judicial processes will soon resolve the legal, political, and more dilemmas which confront modern technological society. The courts, along with other institutions, must face up to the inherent uncertainties of regulation at the frontiers of knowledge and play their part in protecting current and future generations against risks of harm. Judges must, indeed, be post-industrial wise men and women.

NOTES

1. The court subsequently ruled in *American Textile Manufacturers Institute* v. *Donovan* (452 U.S. 490, 1981), the "cotton dust" case, that OSHA is not required to meet a cost-benefit test in setting standards. Justice Brennan's opinion held that "cost-benefit analysis is not required by the statute because feasibility analysis is." This opinion, in contrast to those of the majority in *Industrial Union*, recognizes the hierarchy of values written into the law by Congress, but leaves the threshold-significance test intact. Justice Burger now joined Rehnquist in a dissent holding that the OSH Act is unconstitutionally vague.

2. O'Connor cites Marshall's dissent at p. 16 (slip opinion), and her language closely parallels his. This suggests that a new consensus has emerged in the past year or two.

3. The court's position may soon be tested as OSHA has now promised to issue new permanent standards further limiting exposure to abestos and benzene (*The Wall Street Journal*, June 7, 1983, 7). Ironically, even the Reagan Administration's OSHA is now considering benzene standards as low as 0.5 ppm.

PART III
THREATS TO INSTITUTIONS
FROM MANAGING RISKS

Chapter 5

HIDDEN RISKS IN RISK ASSESSMENT: THE PROBLEM OF TECHNOLOGY'S INSTITUTIONAL IMPACTS
Walter A. Rosenbaum

Editor's Introduction

The papers in this section consider the threats to institutions themselves from attempting to manage risks posed by new technologies to health and the environment. Each of the papers in this section is based on the premise that organizational or political aims are legitimate, and that models of the process for making risk decisions that denigrate or ignore these institutional factors are over-simplified. A related paper by Anthony in the earlier verson of this symposium (1982) shows especially well how organizations' abilities to fulfill the goal of reducing societal risk are compromised by their very efforts to do so. This is surely an argument for a dynamic, iterative risk-assessment process that is designed explicitly to include political and organizational goals.

Rosenbaum introduces the consideration of risks to institutions with a "litany" of problems: lack of contingency plans; lack of resources; and loss of control over the technology itself. The problems we have encountered with old hazardous waste disposal sites illustrate these difficulties as well as the nuclear examples Rosenbaum adduces. His response to these problems is to institute a process that explicitly includes review of effects on institutions of adopting a particular risk control strategy.

The description of problems and the proposal make very clear why adopting a two-stage model of the risk process is not only wrong, but dangerous. The result of our populist heritage is an inherent distrust of government that prevents us from admitting that it is legitimate, even necessary, for institutions to take actions to maintain themselves. The two-stage model embodies this attitude by subordinating the political analysis to the scientific, and by assuming that the scientific can drive the policy outcome. In contrast, Rosenbaum assumes that institutional values are legitimate, and proposes a process—a complex, probably iterative process of more than two-stages—that allows the pursuit of institutional continuity and strength to be balanced against other valid goals.

In twenty years, risk assessment has changed from a political experiment into a federal policy. It is well past time to talk about the risks involved in this risk assessment; a good place to start is federal technology development. Within the last twenty years, Congress has written more than 30 major laws to regulate technological hazards; fifteen of these mandate some form of assessment for public risks associated with a technology's development or proliferaton (Covello and Menkes 1982; Richmond, et al., 1981). Risk assessment programs affecting a wide range of technologies have been further multiplied by administrative regulations such as President Reagan's Executive Order No. 12291, widely interpreted among federal agencies as an encouragement to formal risk assessment during administrative rulemaking. The current profusion of assessment techniques is a beginning toward more responsible federal technology management. For more than a decade, however, there have been warnings that this assessment, despite its growing scientific sophistication, is also becoming an implicit social gamble—dangerous, needless and often willful.

Conventional risk assessment focuses almost exclusively upon the probability, magnitude and acceptability of adverse technological impacts upon human health and the environment (Lowrance 1975, Chapters 1−3). A pervasive flaw in this procedure is a failure to examine routinely and explicitly the impact of technologies upon the institutions responsible for their management or affected by their operation. The implicit gamble is that it doesn't matter. One warning of the cost to such indifference came late in 1971, on 3400 acres of snow-dusted farmland in Cattaraugus County, south of Buffalo, where part of the Nuclear Dream died.

In Cattaraugus County the nation's only commercial nuclear fuel reprocessing plant—the showpiece technology at West Valley intended to advertise the feasibility of commercializing the "back end" of the nuclear fuel cycle—faltered and, four years later, failed. The plant closed in 1971; in September, 1976, the private operator, Nuclear Fuel Services, announced it was vacating the plant for economic reasons and transferring authority for site management to the wholly unprepared State of New York. The plant closing severely disrupted the nation's whole nuclear reprocessing cycle (GAO 1−2).[1] Abandoned at West Valley were more than a half-million gallons of high-level liquid radioactive waste ("radwaste") in two large storage containers, two solid radwaste burial grounds, a spent nuclear fuel storage facility and a contaminated fuel reprocessing plant. This plant must be decontaminated and the surrounding population (more than a million people live relatively close to West Valley) assured protection from these hazards.

Washington and Albany quarreled for almost four years over the responsibility to clean up these hazards. In mid-1982, this squabble and a lack of legal or institutional resources to attack the problems effectively left most conditions at West Valley still unaltered. "Obviously," remarked a New York State official involved in the controversy, "none of the parties to the joint venture contemplated what has happened . . . ." But the fiasco could have been anticipated, as could many other institutional problems characterizing federal technology developments we shall examine. [2]

West Valley's warning is that the interaction between developing technologies and the social institutions they affect—especially public institutions upon which we shall focus—can produce adverse impacts which shall be called "institutional risks." There are risks *to* the institutions and risks to society *from* the institutions involved in technology development. Four of these risks involving public institutions will be examined: (1) the absence of explicit and operational contingency plans for dealing with technological emergencies; (2) the lack of regulatory, financial and technical resources appropriate for dealing with technology failures; (3) the inflation of public costs for technology R&D attributable to incompetent public management; and (4) unanticipated and possibly pernicious alternations of public law and institutions to accommodate a technology's development. All this is an examination in the context of risk assessment of what Edward Wenk has called "social-technical couplets." Complex technologies are so commonly bound to complex social infrastructure that I would change Dorothy Nelkin's perceptive description of nuclear power plants in only one respect. A nuclear power plant not only creates "an interdependence of organizational and technical systems," it *is* such an interdependence (Nelkin 1981, 133). In short, to paraphrase David L. Sills, technology is a social concept (Sills 1981).

After describing the nature of these adverse institutional impacts in federal technology development, the social costs of these risks will be illuminated to emphasize the potential value in examining institutional impacts early in technology development. Finally, issues leading to a possible soluton will be examined: the obstacles to better risk assessment, the substantive design of a prudent institutional impact assessment and the implications for public institutions of such an assessment. The end of analysis ought to be the beginning of a social learning curve, the translation to new institutional and procedural forms of lessons learned from past experience with technology innovation.

A LITANY OF INSTITUTIONAL RISKS

The federal government's most sustained, expensive and complex involvement in technology development over the last four decades has been associated with the development of domestic nuclear power in which Washington has invested at least $13 billion since 1945. It is from this, and to a lesser extent from emerging experience with the development of a domestic synthetic fuels industry, that many important institutional risks in technology development can be defined.

In the last decade, social scientists have become increasingly aware that nuclear technologies, and commercial synfuels facilities as well, have social impacts that ought to be anticipated (Ausness 1979; Kasperson, 1977). Among the institutional risks that ought to be routinely estimated as well are the following:

Risk #1: The Lack of Practical and Explicit Contingency Plans for Technology Failures

Two incidents bracketing the last decade—the failure of the West Valley reprocessing plant and the dangerously close approach to a core "meltdown" at the light water reactor on Three Mile Island (TMI)—illustrate this risk.

None of the governmental entities initially responsible for the operation of West Valley's technology had been willing to create institutional strategies for dealing with a prospective failure. This was most conspicuous in the initial contract negotiated between the private operator and the State of New York (the federal government, while actively encouraging the agreement, was not formally a party). Notes the General Accounting Office study of the confusion attending the plant's abandonment:

> . . .the terms of the contract bear no relationship to the facts as they exist today. [A New York State official] said that the express terms of these 1963 agreements are of little help because the parties at West Valley (including the federal government) contemplated a successful venture and did not specifically address in the contracts their respective liabilities for the radically different situation which exists at West Valley today (General Accounting Office #2, 15).

This negligence begot a technological pariah whose dangers to public health and the environment continued undiminished while quarreling governments and the private contractor dodged responsibiity for the expensive and imperative task of cleaning up the facility. Practically every physical artifact associated with the plant itself is a radwaste. Some of the wastes, including fission products remaining from the spent nuclear fuel rods already reprocessed, will remain dangerous for as long as 20,000 years. During the six years these wastes have languished at West Valley, leaks have been detected in the high-level waste containment structures; experts believe the danger of containment breakdowns will grow until public agencies initiate remedial measures (Bodansky and Schmidt 1976; General Accounting Office, #2).

The nation's most publicized nuclear technology failure, the crisis at Three Mile Island beginning in March, 1978, was described by both major commissions investigating the incident as primarily a failure in institutional management. The conclusion of President Carter's Kemeny Commission, observes David Sills, "have very little to do with [TMI] being an engineering failure . . .[rather] the commission concluded that the accident was the result of social system failure, although it did not use this term" (Sills 1981, 144). The Rogovin Commission appointed by the NRC was more explicit: "The principal deficiencies in commercial reactor safety today are not hardware problems, they are management problems . . . problems that cannot be solved by the additon of a few pipes and valves— or, for that matter, by a resident federal inspector" (Rogovin 1980, 89). It is significant, in light of the Rogovin Commission's emphasis upon institutional management as a problem *generic* to the commercial reactor industry, that the major risk assessment study of reactor safety used by the NRC until 1978, the report of the Rassmussen Commission, did not consider failures of institutional management among the several thousand varieties of "human error" whose contribution to risks in reactor operations it considered.

The lack of adequate contingency planning between public agencies was among the most serious managerial problems revealed at TMI. An "Interagency Radiological Assistance Plan," for instance, purportedly existed to mobilize expert assistance among a multitude of public agencies in case of a core meltdown. But "the existence of this plan was not well known, links between agencies were poorly established, and lines of responsibility were weakly defined" (Nelkin 1981, 139). Stage agencies had no plans for emergency evacuation of residents endangered by a potential core meltdown nor the capability to monitor radiation levels around TMI. An approved agent for protecting the thyroid gland from radioactive iodine, potassium iodide, was not commercially available in quantities sufficient to protect the population around TMI (Gorinson 1982). The Kemeny Commission has recommended that operational evaluation plans by local governments should be required before new construction permits or operating licenses are issued for future nuclear reactors.

Problems associated with the nation's only commercial nuclear fuel reprocessing plant might be considered unique to New York. But 74 licensed nuclear power plants are presently operating and 93 more have construction permits; the risks of institutional planning for nuclear technology management revealed at TMI have, in this perspective, been nationally distributed.

Risk #2: Inadequate Regulatory, Financial and Technical Resources to Deal with Technology Failures

More than contingency planning was lacking at West Valley and TMI. The public institutions responsible, or likely to be responsible, for the management of these technology malfunctions often lacked the resources necessary to implement any adequate long-term management of the damaged technologies. In effect, the technology surprises at TMI and West Valley forced upon the affected public agencies a belated discovery of an incapacity to take actions that would be required in contingency planning. Thus, agencies were forced to inventory their technical and legal resources after the critical events—what adequate contingency planning is supposed to prevent.

When it became obvious, for instance, that the Federal government would have to assume a major role in solving the West Valley problems it became equally clear that Federal authorities were not—and still are not—prepared technically or legally for such an undertaking (General Accounting Office, #3). Among the legal deficiencies for dealing with high-level radwastes, for instance, was Congressional failure to pass legislation mandating a technology for solidifying the high-level wastes because the NRC had not created criteria for such a technology. In deciding how to dispose of the low-level radwastes at West Valley, Federal authorities discovered they lacked such basic information as the source and amount of low-level radwastes generated in the U.S.

One reason it took more than 25 months for the NRC and General Public Utility Corporation (GPU), owner of TMI, to agree upon a decontamination plan for the reactor containment building at TMI-2 was that the NRC had no specific guidelines or criteria relevant to a nuclear accident recovery plan. Rather, NRC staff placed responsibility upon GPU to propose decontamination procedures to which the NRC staff reacted. The absence of an NRC document to guide GPU in disposing of 500,000 gallons of intermediate-level contaminated waste water and 600,000 gallons of high-level radwaste water is only a facet of the technical and legal inadequacies created at TMI. It has been estimated that disposal of all low- to high-level radwastes presently at TMI will require a four-year program to haul 2000 truckloads of such waste over a distance of 2500 miles to Hanford, Washington (Peterson 1982). The NRC and the Department of Energy (DOE) currently face problems in disposing of these wastes similar to those encountered in disposing of radwastes at West Valley.

The void of technical and legal capacity for institutional management of technologies failing at West Valley and TMI is alarming because it prolongs the time during which the public and environment may be exposed to adverse impacts while the magnitude of risk may itself be increased. Another type of institutional risk—the economic mismanagement of technologies through public and private institutional incompetence—creates large economic losses to the public and seems to have existed since the first federal dollar was appropriated for technology research and development (R&D).

Risk #3: Technology Cost Inflation through Incompetent Public Management

Federal technology development is often, if not usually, a spendthrift affair. Budget-busting cost overruns have become federal house style in the development of such diverse technologies as the Apollo space program, the light-water nuclear reactor, solar 'power towers' and—the current champion—the Clinch River Breeder Reactor whose original 1972 estimate of $667 million has now swollen to at least $2.2 billion (General Accounting Office #4). Cost overruns are often the product of unpredictable factors but federal R&D programs in technology have also been afflicted by mismanagement or other deficiencies whose likelihood could have been predicted, and possibly prevented, by adequate assessment of program needs before development. Some of the best current illustrations come from the federal government's efforts to commercialize coal liquefaction and gasificaton. In erly 1975, the Energy Research and Development Administration (ERDA) awarded a contract to Coalcon, a consortium of petrochemical companies, to produce low-BTU clean boiler fuel at a plant to be located at New Athens in Southern Illinois. Two years and $237 million later, ERDA admitted failure and terminated the project. Commented the U.S. Comptroller General's Office: ''The project was plagued by technical and managerial problems from the beginning; failed in its initial phase despite a $10 million (211 percent) cost overrun and a 14½ month slippage'' (General Accounting Office #5, #6). One reason for this failure was ERDA's neglect to investigate the consortium's capability to resolve technical problems early in the project's development (General Accounting Office #6). More recently, the Federal government's effort to produce a pilot plant using an H-Coal process for coal liquefaction is predicted to cost almost 66 percent over original estimates ($296.1 million instead of $178.8 million). One reason for this overrun, according to a GAO investigation, was the Energy Department's haste to award the contract; an agreement ''made before the design scheme for the H-Coal plant was complete'' meant that ''the scope of work to be performed could only be general in nature and estimates had no sound basis'' (General Accounting Office #7). DOE further contributed to the project's soaring overrun by failing to investigate the prime contractor's work schedule, labor requirements and sub-contracting arrangements.

These problems responsible for cost overruns in synfuels R&D, as well as other federal technology R&D, could often be anticipated if probing questions had been asked in advance of contract awards concerning the capabilities of contractors to finish projects. Most lacking was the will to ask such questions.

Risk #4: The Rapid, and Possibly Undesirable, Modification of Public Law or Institutions to Accommodate a Technology's Continuing Development

Public agencies often commit themselves to technology development without explicit, prolonged examination of the long-term legal or institutional changes entailed in such development. Many evolving technologies are driven along their developmental path by politically influential constituencies, large "sunk costs" and powerful public and governmental expectations that acquire the political force to achieve rather rapid changes in public laws or institutions justified as essential to a technology's continuing evolution. Such a political climate is uncongenial to the careful weighing and debating about the implications of such change. Opponents of such change are often thwarted by assertions from a technology's proponents that failure to make the desied accommodation will debilitate, if not preclude, the promise of the technology.

A case in point is the Price-Anderson Act, passed in 1957 by Congress to limit the liability of private utilities to $560 million from a single nuclear reactor accident. Wood's paper, in this volume, discusses the genesis and history of the $560 million figure, the inadequacy of which is illustrated by the fact that the estimated consumer liability or clean up cost of TMI-2 is between one and two billion dollars. This means a law intended to induce private utility investment in nuclear power may have the effect of forcing consumers to bear more than half the cost of the technology's mismanagement. The Act was defended by Congress and the Atomic Energy Commission (AEC) as essential to induce private utility investment in nuclear power plants and to permit the AEC to fulfill its Congressional mandate to promote nuclear power in the U.S. (Nader and Abbotts 1979). Nuclear technology continues to create pressures for statutory accommodation to its developmental needs—a sort of legal *lebensraum*—which may mean significant alterations in traditiona American concepts of law. For instance, the current failure of commercial nuclear fuel reprocessing may eventually require that the Federal government preempt the designation and administration of low- and high-level nuclear waste sites and thereby override the will of state and local officials and their constituents. Would such an alteration in existing Federal-State collaboration on radwaste issues constitute an unacceptable change in the statutory basis of Federalism?

Institutional changes created, or strongly favored, by technology development ought to be pondered with equal concern at the outset of technology development. The experience at TMI strongly suggests, for example, that nuclear reactor failures—or the failure of any new or exotic technology—may create a de facto displacement of public authority from elected public officials and other legally constituted entities to a cadre of scientific experts able to understand and respond to the technological problems arising from the technological crisis. "The scientist's expanding influence following the TMI accident," writes Dorothy Nelkin, "suggests the heavy dependence on the judgment of an expert elite whenever problems of technological risk arise. For power tends to gravitate to those who can manage the critical information. As problems of risk assume increased policy importance, this tendency to augment the power of expertise raises serious questions about political legitimacy, exacerbating existing tensions over democratic control technology and deepening public distrust" (Nelkin 1981, 139). In a different perspective, most local U.S. governments have no ability to identify, or monitor, the hazardous and toxic sludges or gases associated with synfuels technology. Lacking such technical capability, to what extent does this remove from local government an effective regulatory influence over the conduct of synfuels facilities and force such government to depend upon federal agencies, or scientific cadres, to make decisions about major technological facilities within their own jurisdictions that vitally affect the health of local citizens?

Such a litany of risks drawn from national experience with a few technologies, and then primarily from technology failures, constitutes a limited observation of technology development within the U.S. But, as Robert Kates remarks, risk assessment must be opportunistic and it is often only through technological crises that the social capacities to deal with technologies are fully revealed. Moreover, the risks described, even if they characterized only a small proportion of the technological innovations through public management, would merit careful assessment because the public and private costs of institutional failures can be severe.

THE COST OF INSTITUTIONAL FAILURES

The institutional risks of technology development ought to be considered as much a matter of public finance as social theory. Indeed, institutional risk assessment could be considered a dimension of benefit/cost analysis if one observes the public cost from institutional mismanagement of technology.

High public costs of institutional failures in technology development arise from several sources:

1. *Orphaned technologies and technology sites*. Estimates suggest the cost of adequately disposing of the abandoned West

Valley site will be $42 million to $1.1 billion—when a comprehensive disposal plan is finally adopted (General Accounting Office, June 1980). Appalachia is a national showcase of institutional failure in strip-mine management. The region's hills and hollows are covered by more than 250,000 acres of "orphan" spoil banks which continue to pollute land and water. Between 1950 and 1977 nothing was done to treat these spoil banks. Today, adequate restoration, if possible, may exceed $1 billion (Office of Technology Assessment 1978).

2. *Phantom technologies.* A delay of years, or decades, in the development of technologies, may be due to institutional mismanagement. If these technologies are a phase in a developmental sequence—for instance, a segment in an integrated R&D program to commercialize an energy source—short-term costs are compounded by disruptions of the whole program schedule. Early federal failure to develop demonstration plants using Solvent Refined Coal technology for coal liquefaction have delayed that program perhaps a decade, adding between 50 and 150 percent to commercialization costs.

3. *Private sector spillovers.* The losses to individuals, business and corporations with an economic stake in technology development can often be substantial when the technology fails. The failure of TMI-2, for instance, involved local lost wages of $5.7–$8.3 million in manufacturing, $2.8–$3.8 million in the nonmanufacturing sector. Additionally, $6 to $8 million in lost tourist revenues and $1 million in agriculture losses should be counted (Nelkin 1981, 133). Often the true magnitude of economic damage from technology failures is distinguished when only the losses of public investment are publicized.

The costs of technology failure soar further because inadequate institutional responses breed bureaucratic and politicized problem solving. The "lag time" from crisis to management is inflated by public agencies groping and laboring toward solutions through bureaucratic routines. Moreover, missing institutional strategies for technology failures usually mean that every major element in the subsequent formation of a management program—legal, technical and economic issues—are debated, and bargained, between the affected public and private agencies. Issues that might have been competently debated in advance of a technology problem or agreements that might have been quietly settled outside the glare of publicity are precluded. Solutions to technical issues often prevail less for scientific merit than for political feasibility. In West Valley, for instance, sound technical and economic reasons existed for treating all major radwaste problems in a single comprehensive plan but this proved politically impossible (General Accounting Office, #2). At the very least, political bargaining prolongs the time for resolving technology issues.

The economic penalties entailed in poor technology management would alone seem sufficient to awaken public agencies to a greater sensitivity about the institutional implications of technology development. But at a time when governments at all levels seem increasingly risk averse in dealing with health or environmental impacts of technology they remain risk tolerant, and often insensible, to institutional risks. The reason, I think, lies not in the difficulty of knowing what questions to ask about institutional impacts but in political and bureaucratic inhibition to the asking. These powerful inhibitions are deeply rooted in the political philosophy of officials operating in an open, democratic society—so rooted that a high tolerance for institutional risk in technology development may be an inevitable social cost for a liberal, democratic social order.

CREATING BETTER INSTITUTIONAL ASSESSMENT

U.S. District Court Judge David Bazelon, a jurist experienced and perceptive in technology litigation, recently remarked that a major risk in federal risk assesment remained a "refusal to face the hard questions created by a lack of knowledge" (Bazelon 1979, 279). Why are the institutions which should be adept in assessing institutional problems in technology development—the whole panoply of Congressional committees, regulatory agencies, Cabinet departments and White House offices nurturing technologies in the U.S.—so often maladept? More particularly, why do they so often remain untroubled by their lack of information about the institutional implications of their decisions? Partially, they are impeded by the political benefit/cost calculus associated with different assessment strategies. Partially, the problem is structural.

The Obstacles

Short-term forces drive governmental programs, no matter how ambitiously they may be tethered to future objectives. Considerations of immediate electoral advantage, near-term budget impacts, public reaction or bureaucratic consequences are, among other factors, routinely compelling considerations for elective and bureaucratic officials responsible for technology management. The political costs of prudent institutional assessment in technology development are likely to be immediate, the benefits deferred. The advantages to avoiding such assessment are likely to be immediate, the cost deferred. It is a political calculus that strongly favors avoiding institutional assessment.

Three short-term costs of assessing institutional impacts from technology development, in particular, are obvious to public officials. First, an assessment can become an early warning system, not primarily for the mass public but to the many organized, attentive publics that might mobilize to change substantially a technology program whose implications may be more fully and tangibly revealed. That is, institutional assessments are likely to *create* opposition to the technologies they affect. Second, institutional assessments can quickly change a distributive program into a regulatory one. Faced with revelations of possible institutional problems or the need for institutional restructuring to manage emerging technologies, public officials may feel compelled to constrain the program's distributive rewards—they can no longer play unfettered the role of political entrepreneur trading distributive benefits for political support—and instead limit economic benefits to those public or private recipients whose capacities for technology management better conform to requirements revealed by institutional assessment. Finally, institutional assessment is likely to reveal institutional problems regarded by the institutions involved as an indictment of their competence and a threat to their various constituencies. Political conflict and polarization are almost inevitable; coalition building in support of the technology program is impeded.

In contrast, the consequences of neglected institutional analysis, however potentially severe, can easily seem diffuse and deferrable to officials. These problems can be considered later—if they occur—while the rewards of a technology's development may be immediately savored. Deferred costs are further tolerated because many prospective institutional problems will seem diffuse and unpredictable. The public, various electoral constituencies and pressure groups may not readily grasp the implications of a future institutional problem but can readily appreciate the immediate, tangible benefits of governmental spending on a technology program. It was this willingness to trade short-term benefits for long-term risks that prompted Joseph Coates, a former high-ranking official in the Congressional Office of Technology Assessment to complain that short-term forces dominating technology development ''almost never accurately reflect the ultimate changes that technology will bring'' (Coates 1982, 27).

All this implies that an instinctive official aversion to knowing the consequences of decisions—almost a willful ignorance—rather than naivete or inexperience often leads public officials to neglect the institutional consequences of their technology decisions. If so, it may be an inevitable liability of technology planning in a democracy. This behavior is doubtless encouraged by open public access to governmental deliberations, by the desire of White House and Congressional officials to build and maintain electoral support, and by the ability of public bureaucracies and private interests to mobilize politically when their stake in technology development is jeopardized. In short, it arises from the conditions of government conducted in an open and democratic society. Exploring the institutional implications of technology development candidly and carefully would seem more easily conducted through cloistered deliberations where participants are liberated from constant preoccupation with the impact of their discoveries on electoral constituencies, or public opinion, or other institutions capable of battling publically over the result of deliberations.

Beyond short-term forces, a second obstacle to better institutional analysis is what Coates has called the bureaucratic "lack of experience, tools, and motivation for thinking in system terms" (Coates 1982, 26). Many proposals for technology development, assessments of technological risks, and evaluations of technology performance originate within the federal bureaucracy. Congress and the White House, moreover, depend heavily upon bureaucratic expertise for the information base upon which continuing decisions about technology programs are made. Bureaucracies are usually concerned with their own mission, with protecting budgets and clientele, with preserving or enhancing Congressional or White House influence—preoccupations which deflect attention from a thorough examination of the systemic impacts of technology decisions over which they may wield substantial influence. The same insensitivity to system impacts can often be observed in perspective of the quasi-public scientific and economic institutions which constitute a shadow bureaucracy in governmental technology development—the institutions upon which Congress and the administrative branch often rely to provide "outside" and "objective" technology assessments when controversies arise. For instance, two private Washington institutions highly influential in governmental technology assessment—Resources for the Future and the National Academy of Sciences—recently published comprehensive studies of future U.S. energy needs with only a terse and oblique mention of institutional management problems (Schurr 1979; National Academy of Sciences 1979).

Another obstacle to better institutional analysis, having much the same effect upon bureaucracy but a very different cause, is the strong inhibition in U.S. political culture against institutions candidly and publicly seeking to preserve or advance their own institutional fortunes. That governmental institutions do promote their own organizational interests is, of course, common knowledge. But they must usually do it covertly or deceptively, finding whatever language and logic will move political forces in the desired direction without explicitly and unapologetically discussing the implications of law for their own survival. It is difficult, in such a political climate, for public agencies to overcome the populist bias against government sufficiently to explore at length, and with full disclosure, the full implications of technology developments to themselves.

If greater governmental attention to the institutional implications of technology development is to be achieved, what then can be done? One possible answer is to attack the problem simultaneously at both bureaucratic and legislative levels by action-forcing mechanisms that compel decision-makers to acknowledge and evaluate a full range of possible institutional impacts of technology decisions. The primary purpose of such a procedure would be to reveal as clearly and explicitly as possible the nature of possible institutional impacts, and the probability of such impacts. As with other types of risk assessment, the responsibility for deciding upon the *acceptability* of various impact scenarios should rest with the Congressional committees, White House officials, bureaucratic agencies or other governmental institutions ultimately responsible for authorizing the development and dissemination of technologies. But the identification and description of such impacts should be, insofar as possible, sufficiently broad to prevent the suppression of important issues. In brief, decision-makers should be compelled to face up to the full institutional implications of their technology decisions and to explicitly decide upon their acceptability.

Some Proposals

Several strategies might be followed to force greater federal attention to institutional problems in technology development. A conservative approach would be to encourage the White House, or relevant federal departments and regulatory agencies, to interpret a number of existing requirements for risk assessment in technology related programs. The statutory language of the Toxic Substance Control Act (1974), the Outer Continental Shelf Lands Acts (1976), the Occupational Safety and Health Act (1974) and several other federal laws would seem to permit such an analysis under their broadly defined risk assessment requirements (Ricci and Molton 1981). The language in these statutes is similar to that in the Federal Insecticide, Fungicide and Rodenticide Act which permits the suspension of pesticides when there is "unreasonable risk to man or the environment, taking into account the economic, *social* and environmental costs and benefits . . . ." (italics added); "social" in this context would seem broad enough to embrace the sort of impacts here discussed. President Reagan's Executive Order No. 12291 urges federal regulatory agencies to use a "regulatory impact analysis" in deciding whether to adopt new regulations or revise older ones; this "regulatory impact analysis" is to include "evaluation of effects that cannot be quantified in monetary terms"—language sufficiently ambiguous to permit institutional impact analysis in the regulatory process for technology development.

A more difficult but more incisive approach would be a legislative and administrative mandate for institutional assessment which assures uniformity of language and substantive requirements among all officials and agencies involved. Such a strategy might include the following administrative procedures:

1. The enactment of legislation requiring institutional impact assessment for all administrative proposals, policy decisions, or regulations having a major impact on the development, utilization or commercialization of technologies. This assessment would be analogous in its implementation to Section 102(2)(C) of the National Environmental Policy Act (1969) which mandates an "environmental impact statement" for major administrative decisions affecting the human or natural environment.

2. The requirement that such an institutional impact assessment must include at least the following substantive provisions:
   a. Identification of the principal public and private institutions responsible for the management of a technology during whatever portion of its development is affected by the policy, proposal or regulation.
   b. Projection of institutional needs and resources for a technology's management on a multi-year basis that tracks the technology through the full sequence of development affected by the proposed policy or regulation.
   c. Evaluation of resources required, and those actually available, for such institutions to deal with a full range of possible technology failures or malfunctions. This examination should include explicit discussion of contingency plans neded, and those existing, to deal with such problems.
   d. Examination of possible changes in public institutions or public law which may be required to accommodate the development of technologies over the period "tracked" in part (b).
   e. Statement of the probabilties associated with any adverse institutional consequences revealed in parts (a) through (d).
   f. Statement of alternative strategies for dealing with such institutional problems as may be revealed by the assessment.

3. Review of these assessments by the White House Office of Science and Technology Policy, or another White House science office, in a manner similar to review of environmental impact statements by the President's Commission on Environmental Quality.

Experience with the National Environmental Policy Act (1969) indicates that Congress is far more enthusiastic about prescribing impact assessments for administrative agencies than it is in creating them for itself. However, two Congressional staff agencies presently have considerable experience in technology assessment, including institutional analysis: the General Accounting Office (GAO) and the Office of Technology Assessment (OTA). Neither agency, however, has in its charter language sufficiently broad and explicit to permit institutional impact assessment routinely for Congressional legislation. Nonetheless, the capacity for institutional assessment is present in such staff agencies. A legislative approach to institutional assessment built upon this staff base might include:

1. The enactment of legislation mandating that an assessment similar to that described above be required for all Congressional legislation authorizing the development of new technologies through federal R&D and for all legislation creating significant changes in technologies currently supported by federal R&D appropriations.

2. The provision that such assessments may be made by administrative agencies in the case of proposals originating with them. For proposals initiated in Congress, such assessments might be performed by the GAO, the OTA, or an office created particularly for this purpose.

A still more ambitious program could be designed along lines suggested by legislation introduced by Republican Congressmen William Wampler (Va.) and Donald Ritter (Pa.); both bills would require the creation of special science advisory panels to consult with regulatory agencies by mandate on the health and environmental risks of scientific, technological and related decisions. Institutional assessment could be added as another category of risk analysis. Such a new scientific advisory panel should be created as an independent agency or an advisory commission within the Executive Office of the President to assure the independence of viewpoint desired by the legislators. Such an approach, however, holds no assurance that Congress would avail itself of the science panel's expertise in its own deliberations.

The first three proposals have the advantage of requiring relatively moderate changes within the federal government, particularly if Congressional impact assessments are conducted through the GAO or OTA. The most innovative institutional changes, beyond the passage of the appropriate legislation, would be the development within bureaucratic and Congressional staff agencies of a capability for institutional analysis. This would probably require the use of specialists in law, political science, sociology and the humanities (including philosophy and religion). There is already a precedent for the use of sorts for the enlistment of these specialists in the federal government's use of ethicists and philosophers on the National Science Foundation's Recombinant DNA Review Panel. Also required would be the creation of appropriate review procedures to assure that institutional assessments are considered by decison-makers at the most important stages of policymaking.

Do Governments Learn?

The most immediate obstacle to the development of better institutional impact assessment for federally managed technologies is clearly political feasibility. Given the enormous political costs associated with such assessments at an early stage in technology development, there is likely to be a lack of political will, or a public clamor for such assessment, in the absence of some arresting crisis which points unambiguously to the need for better institutional management of emerging technologies. This is, perhaps, an unfortunate but inevitable price for doing technological business in a democracy. But it is not too early to begin assiduously propagating the ideas of institutional impact assessment within Congress, the Executive establishment, Congressional staff agencies and the scientific community—that is, wherever technical—scientific issues are joined to the governmental structure. A further step in the cultivation of a political opinion climate more congenial to institutional assessments would be the inclusion of institutional management issues as part of the professional education of scientists, technologists, public officials and others likely to assume responsibility for technology management in the future. Nor is it too early to begin acquainting the next generation of voters with the problems of technology management through courses, perhaps introduced as early as the high school curriculum, which include such an issue in basic science education. Stated somewhat differently, it is when technology development is defined as much a social issue as a scientific one that the full implications of its management, and the many governmental problems it creates, can be appreciated and appropriately introduced in the education of those who will inherit the responsibility, and the liability, for future technology developments.

NOTES

1. The general accounting office has issued a series of reports on West Valley and related topics. They are listed here and referred to in the text by number. (For example, this reference indicates the June and October 1980 reports).

#1 *U.S. Congress, General Accounting Office. Further Analysis of Issues at Western New York Nuclear Service Center.* Report No. EMD-81-5 (October 23, 1980).

#2 *Ibid. Status of Efforts to Clean Up the Shut-down Western New York Nuclear Service Center.* Report No. EMD-80-69 (June 6, 1980).

#3 *Ibid. The Problem of Disposing of Nuclear Low-Level Waste: Where Do We Go From Here?* Report No. EMD-80-68 (March 31, 1980).

#4 U.S. Congress, General Accounting Office. *The Clinch River Breeder Reactor: Should Congress Continue to Fund It?* Report No. EMD-79-62 (May 7, 1979).

#5 *Ibid. First Federal Attempt to Demonstrate a Synthetic Fossil Energy Technology: A Failure.* Report No. EMD-77-59 (June 6, 1977).

#6 *Ibid. Fossil Energy Research, Development, and Demonstration: Opportunities for Change.* Report No. EMD-78-57 (September 18, 1978).

#7 *Ibid. Controlling Federal Costs for Coal Liquefaction Program Hinges On Management and Contracting Improvements.* Report No. PSAD-81-19 (February 4, 1981).

2. U.S Congress, House Committee on Interior and Insular Affairs, Subcomittee on Energy and Environment. *Remedial Action At West Valley, N.Y.* 96th Congress, 1st Session, May 31, 1979. Serial No. 96-12. 90.

Chapter 6

PUBLIC POLICY AND THE IMPONDERABLE NUMBER: INSURANCE FOR NUCLEAR ACCIDENTS
William C. Wood

Editor's Introduction

Rosenbaum and other commentators often suggest new procedures with built-in checks and balances to enable institutions to manage risk better. A different response is to simplify. Unfortunately, there are also institutional risks in simplification.

Kraft's respondents discussed the problems that arise when policymakers take one number from a complex analysis and use it as a summary of the whole. In another study, Wood (1983) has shown how the Nuclear Regulatory Commission has committed this very error. Wood's article here makes a slightly different but related point—having arrived at a single number, which did probably summarize a combination of political and technical factors at the time it was first derived, policymakers allowed it to take on an existence independent of the conditions of its birth. The iterative model I proposed in the introduction assumes that significant changes in scientific (or political) knowledge will trigger a reexamination of existing risk policy. When the process fails, new information is not reflected in altered policies. This in itself poses a risk to institutions.

The article makes another important contribution to this book because it is the only one directly to discuss insurance as a form of risk control. (Graham discusses it indirectly.) Insurance has long been used as a means of spreading risk, thereby reducing the monetary consequences to each individual subscriber. Insurance does nothing, however, to reduce the physical effects, probability, or incidence of risk, and we have implicitly assumed that most government policies will be addressed to these aspects of risk control. We also know that the availability of insurance makes people less worried about the risk itself, enhancing rather than inhibiting risk-reducing behavior. Wood's paper raises yet another disturbing question about using the availability of government-sponsored insurance to signal citizens that an activity is desirable and acceptably safe.

A relatively recent challenge to policymakers and institutions is that posed by the low-probability catastrophe. Hazards involving high probabilities of low consequences, such as those of automobile travel, are familiar and accepted. Hazards involving low probabilities of catastrophic consequences—nuclear power providing a prime example—are much harder to deal with.

The challenge of the low-probability catastrophe is a modern one, since only in recent history have there existed technologies, such as nuclear power, that present the threat of catastrophic maximum consequences. (For other technologies posing similar hazards, see Solomon and Okrent, 1977). As an illustration, the worst accident that one can imagine when cars collide is within the bounds of comprehension and experience. The worst accident that one can imagine at a nuclear plant would be a disaster unprecedented in history.

In many ways, the decisions on controlling a one-in-a-thousand risk of a $100,000 auto accident are different from the decisions on controlling the one-in-a-billion risk of a $100 billion catastrophe. The risk of the auto accident is easily translated into a private insurance premium equal to $100 plus the administrative costs of offering the policy. The company insuring a thousand drivers can count on taking in $100,000 plus administrative costs each year. It would then pay out about $100,000 in the one such accident expected to occur each year. Existing private institutions are well geared toward handling such risks.

But existing institutions are not well equipped to cope with catastrophe. The private insurer prepared to take on a one-in-a-billion risk of a $100 billion catastrophe, if such an insurer existed, could not confidently charge the analogous premium of $100 plus administrative costs. *Over a billion years the premium of $100 billion* would pay for itself.—But what if the catastrophe occurred in the first 500 years? The premiums paid in would form a fund of only $50,000 and the insurer would be out more than $99 billion. Of course, expressing the problem this way only highlights the absurdity of assuming that any existing institution will be around 500 years from now, let alone a billion years from now.

Just as existing institutions are not well equipped to cope with low-probability events, neither are individuals. As Kunreuther (1976, 1978) and Kahneman, Slovic, and Tversky (1982) show, individuals are poorly informed about the probabilities and consequences of such events, and ignorant about what financial protection does exist. As a result, in one specific case considered by Kunreuther, individuals made decisions about buying flood insurance that could only be considered irrational by observing economists.

Unlike the other contributions in this volume, which consider means of controlling actual technological risk, the emphasis of this chapter is on the role of insurance policy in spreading risk. Insurance, whether public or private, has as its primary purpose the distribution of risk across a larger group than the victims of an accident. Under an appropriately constructed insurance plan, everybody pays a small amount in premiums or taxes so that no one will suffer a large financial loss. Those who suffer financial loss in the event of an accident receive some compensaton and are better off than they would have been in the absence of an insurance program. Even those who pay the premiums or taxes can be better off in an *ex ante* sense because of the peace of mind that comes with protection from financial loss.

Therefore, insurance can be of great benefit in controlling the consequences of risks to individuals, even if it does not by itself control the technological risk. However, government policy on insurance can be more than a decision to subsidize, regulate, or even offer directly, insurance coverage. Another fundamental aspect of government policy on insurance, sure to arise in the case of new and poorly understood hazards, stems from the fact that what coverage the government offers may be the only coverage offered. Government efforts may implicitly or explicitly dissuade private insurers from offering coverage. Thus the government will be not only the insurer but also the sole insurer; and because of its actions other coverage may not be offered.

In such a case, the overall effect of government policy may not be to spread risk broadly—as in traditional insurance—but in fact to concentrate the bearing of risk. If the government offers sharply limited coverage and knows that additional private insurance will not be available, then it may actually be decreasing rather than increasing opportunities for the wide spread of risk essential to true insurance programs.

When one considers only the presence or absence of an insurance program, its presence may be taken as a sign that a given activity is acceptably safe. Otherwise, why would the insurer—public or private—be willing to take on the burden of potential claims? As will become evident, the presence of government insurance for nuclear power plants played a role in signaling to the public the government's message that the technology was acceptably safe. The government's program also provided for some of the risk-spreading benefits of insurance. What is not so widely recognized is that, since the government knew that total coverage would be limited to a fixed amount that was small in relation to the potential claims, the government also could have been taken as sending a pessimistic signal on the safety of nuclear power. The availability of insurance normally is taken to make people less worried about the risk itself, making them less willing to engage in risk-reducing behavior. However, when the amount of insurance is severely limited, the mere fact of its presence may not have this important secondary effect. The case presented in this paper illustrates this point.

We have seen that individuals may be ill-informed about risks and that the potential of low-probability catastrophe presents special challenges to private insurers. In such circumstances it is natural that government insurance would be proposed. If any institution can take on the very large portfolio of low-probability risks implied by modern technologies such as nuclear power, it is the government. And if those low probabilities are correctly assessed most, if not all, future generations will get the benefits of the technology without suffering the catastrophe. If the catastrophe does occur, at least the government program will perform the traditional role of insurance by spreading the burden after the fact across a large group of citizens.

This paper examines these questions through a study of a specific aspect of the goverment's actions in insurance for the offsite damages of nuclear power plant accidents: the amount of coverage to be provided. This amount was set at $560 million more than 25 years ago and remains $560 million today. The way in which this figure was derived and its continued use over a long period illustrate some of the risks of resisting change in risk control policies.

BACKGROUND ON NUCLEAR LIABILITY ISSUES

There is no doubt that the worst imaginable nuclear accident would be quite severe. The very operation of reactors generates radioactive products which are harmful to human lives and property; these radioactive products have inherent energy capable of transporting them across the countryside if they are not properly confined. Complete releases of reactors' radioactive products could kill thousands of people, cause billions of dollars' worth of property damage, and contaminate large areas of land (AEC 1957; NRC 1975; WASH 740 Update; Interior 1982).[1]

It is therefore well established that nuclear power poses a possibility of a catastrophe, and it may be that the probability is very low. Surely policymakers must think the probability is quite low, for otherwise it never would have been seriously proposed to allow the possibility of such consequences. Technical studies of the probability of accidents, however, are by their very nature speculative. A particular difficulty with a very low probability is that it cannot be verified in a policy-relevant time period. For an ordinary accident believed to have a probability of one in ten per year, a decade or two of data would provide reasonable confidence. For some of the important probabilities from technical studies of nuclear accidents, it would take perhaps millions of years to have reasonable confidence.[2] In summary, the risk of nuclear power consists of potentially catastrophic consequences occurring with probabilities that are quite uncertain and also may be very small.

No provisions for liability coverage were contained in the original legislation providing for private participation in nuclear power, the Atomic Energy Act of 1954. This legislation ended the government monopoly that had been preserved since the origins of nuclear technology in World War II. The Act viewed nuclear power not only as an energy source, but as a Cold War battleground on which the Soviets had to be defeated. Policymakers were concerned that the Soviets might be first to build a nuclear reactor in an underdeveloped country, thus advancing global communism (JCAE 1956, 216).

By the 1956 opening of hearings on insuring nuclear power plants, it was widely assumed that rapid nuclear development was in the public interest. Thus witnesses saw the lack of insurance at low rates only as a roadblock that could stand in the way of a vital program:

> The purpose of this indemnity program is to get the private atomic energy industry underway because the country needs that industry and needs it desperately (JCAE 1956, 239).

> Certainly in the beginning we would have to give heavy weight to the criteria of being sure that the total of our charge does not defeat the program (JCAE 1956, 14).

Policymakers, then, were not interested in the level or cost of coverage as a separate matter, but instead were concerned that nuclear development not be delayed. The decision process was far different from the rational technical calculation of risk followed by a completely separate set of value judgments on safety (as in Lowrance 1976). Without any credible technical information, policymakers had decided nuclear power presented an acceptable risk. Their only task now was to get utilities to proceed with nuclear construction. It was only in the process of overcoming utilities' reluctance to proceed that technical risk assessments were ordered. In 1956, insurers were reluctant to offer liability coverage for nuclear power and utilities said they would not proceed without coverage. The eventual answer was the Price-Anderson Act of 1957.[4] This Act limited liability to the $560 million figure already mentioned and provided government insurance for $500 million of the total. The government insurance was provided in return for a token fee intended to cover the government's administration costs only (JCAE 1974, 34).

WHY $560 MILLION?

How did the figure of $560 million arise and survive until private insurers were willing to offer $60 million of coverage, but no more. As for the government's participation, the chairman of the Joint Committee on Atomic Energy (JCAE) suggested that half a billion dollars would not disturb the government budget unduly or frighten the public by suggesting the possibility of large damages:

> In suggesting $500 million, I was trying to see if we could not get some figure which would not frighten the country or the Congress to death and still solve the problem which the producers of parts face, and which the fabricator of the entire reactor faces, and which the operator of that reactor would eventually face once he puts it in operation (JCAE 1956, 123). I am only trying to see if we cannot find something that will take care of the insurance needs and at the same time be able to be carried into law and not disturb anybody who is worried about the budget situation (JCAE 1956, 121).

So emerged the $560 million figure—not as the outcome of an analysis of the insurance question, but as the sum of private coverage plus an amount presumed not to disturb the government budget or frighten citizens.

This case raises in a somewhat different form the question that Graham (this volume) considers. Congress had reason to believe that the social benefits of nuclear power would strongly outweigh its costs, but also believed it was faced with a citizenry that could not fully understand this. Since people are likely to overestimate the risks of something unfamiliar, Congress had an incentive to provide information that would belittle those dangers. Provision of insurance sent a comforting signal, since many people would presume that the government wouldn't provide such assurances unless it was convinced that there was a very low probability of having to pay. This strategy can backfire, however; if people find that they were misled, they will distrust the responsible institutions still more. That has indeed happened in the case of nuclear power.

At this point in its hearings, the JCAE turned to the available evidence on how large a nuclear accident's damages might be, in order to consider whether $560 million would be an adequate level of protection. An initial study seemed favorable. Preliminary calculatons by the Atomic Energy Commission (AEC) showed that the maximum damages from a nuclear accident would be $200 million. JCAE members did not explore the origins of the number, the weaknesses of the estimate, or the possible uncertainties. They seemed quite willing to adopt $200 million as a bottom-line figure which justified their policy actions—precisely the sort of reaction that Kraft reports in his study in this volume. For a time, the criterion for the adequacy of insurance coverage was that it exceed the damages of the maximum credible accident—a standard easily met by the proposed $560 million pool of coverage (JCAE 1956, 54).

However a confusion between electrical and thermal kilowatts caused an error in the AEC calculations, and the correct number from that study should have been $600 million. The error was corrected in a letter from the AEC, but that letter was accepted for the record without comment or any consideration of revising the liability level (JCAE 1956, 376). In addition, the incorrect $200 million figure was used again in the JCAE hearings, months after the corrections had been made (JCAE 1957, 217).

When hearings resumed the next year, a new study on the maximum consequences of a nuclear accident was available. This study, from the Brookhaven National Laboratory, made it clear that $560 million would not cover the maximum credible accident. The study indicated a serious accident could cause 3,400 deaths and 43,000 injuries, as well as $7 billion in property damage (AEC 1957). Results of the study were released to the JCAE in an open hearing March 25, 1957, but no AEC witness was questioned about the methods or findings of the study. No revision of the coverage level was proposed.[5] Here policymakers were ignoring scientific findings which pointed in the ''wrong'' directon, after earlier having been quite willing to use scientific findings when it seemed the maximum damages would be $200 million.

If numbers ever take on a life of their own, the $560 million figure did. It survived two renewals of Price-Anderson, even in the face of evidence that nuclear accident consequences had grown in real terms and in the face of continued inflation that cut the real value of $560 million to less than half the amount. The initial Price-Anderson law was to expire after 10 years, when it was hoped that experience would indicate to insurers and the public that its provisions were no longer needed (JCAE 1956, 86). After eight years of experience, however, little had changed and a 10-year extension of Price-Anderson was sought. The Brookhaven Report was tentatively revised in 1964—65 to take account of the increased size of reactors then being designed and built. The revision showed that an accident at the new larger reactors could cause consequences far more severe than those estimated in the original report: 45,000 deaths, 70,000 – 100,000 injuries and $17 billion in property damage.[6]

The JCAE did not seek out the revised study, at least for its public hearings. The JCAE heard only vague testimony from an AEC commissioner that if the Brookhaven Report were updated, ''the damages would certainly not be less'' (JCAE 1965, 20). The revised study was not disclosed until a Freedom of Information Act request forced its release in 1973 (JCAE 1975, 299).

Price-Anderson came up for a second renewal in 1974-1975. Again, policymakers were nagged by the question of whether the coverage level was appropriate. On the one hand, they wanted a dollar amount that would cover even the worst accident. On the other hand, they wanted a coverage level that could comfortably be provided through private insurance and government indemnity. This ambivalence is reflected in a statement by Senator Joseph Montoya during questioning of environmentalist Chauncey Kepford:

> Senator Montoya. We do not have any actuarial basis for saying it should be $200 million. We don't have any actuarial basis for saying it should be $125 million. We are trying to use common sense. We are appealing to you witnesses to help us try to resolve this matter and to provide a ceiling that will be realistic, that will be in line with any possible disaster that might occur.

> Dr. Kepford. Price-Anderson does not in any way, shape or form do that; not with liability limitaton, not with providing $560 million (JCAE 1975, 147).

For the 1974−75 hearings Congress had access to a new study on nuclear reactor accident consequences. This study (NRC 1975), known variously as the *Reactor Safety Study,* WASH-1400, and the "Rasmussen Report," provided no assurance that maximum accident consequences would be less than $560 million. In fact, the worst accident it considered had damages of $14 billion, not counting any awards for loss of life or health (NRC 1975, 83).

The JCAE did not wait for the final verson of the study for its hearings and action on the coverage level. A preliminary conclusion was that the chance of a serious accident was between one in a million and one in a billion per year, and the JCAE acted on the basis of the preliminary conclusion (JCAE 1974, 651). The JCAE reported the extension of the $560 million coverage level unaware (for the record) that peer groups of scientists still had serious reservations about the methodology and findings of the *Reactor Safety Study* (Kendall 1977).

Two aspects of the study were in fact severely criticized by scientists. First the model estimating the biological consequences of various radiation releases was considered to be excessively optimistic. Second, the concept for estimating probabilities was logically flawed. The method involved trying to list all the sources that could initiate a nuclear accident, then assgning probabilities to these events and the succeeding ones that would have to occur for an accident to take place. Each omission would also bias downward the overall estimated probabilities.

Despite these problems, it was the preliminary *Reactor Safety Study* results that were used to justify the smaller real level of coverage inherent in the still-unchanged $560 million level of coverage. Three years later, the study was withdrawn by the Nulear Regulatory Commission because it had been discredited by peer review. The inadequacy of the figure became still clearer when a new study was published shortly thereafter that showed that very unfavorable conditions at a poor site could lead to $314 billion in property damage.

The $560 million figure also survived a review by the U.S. Supreme Court. In a case brought by a North Carolina environmental group, a District Court had ruled that "the amount of recovery is not rationally related to the potential losses" (*Duke Power Co.* v. *Carolina Environmental Study Group,* et al., 431 F. Supp. 222, 1977). The Supreme Court ruled, however, that the $560 million figure was reasonable. The Court was impressed with "expert appraisals" indicating an accident causing more than $560 million would be highly unlikely, and considered it likely that Congress would compensate disaster victims in any event (438 U.S. 85, 1978). The Court added an intriguing assessment of the possibility of setting an appropriate coverage level:

> Given our conclusion that in general limiting liability is an acceptable method for Congress to utilize in encouraging the private development of electric energy by atomic power, candor requires acknowledgement that whatever ceiling figure is selected will, of necessity, be arbitrary in the sense that any choice of a figure based on imponderables like those at issue here can always be so characterized (438 U.S. 86, 1978).

THINKING ABOUT THE APPROPRIATE COVERAGE LEVEL

As the law currently stands, provision of nuclear insurance has been changed so that the nuclear utilities provide the bulk of the coverage through a pooling arrangement. The level of coverage remains at $560 million. The coverage level will be adjusted upward in the future, but not in line with a price index measuring the rate of inflation. Instead, the coverage level will increase $5 million per reactor each time a new reactor comes on line (JCAE 1975, 25−34). As a result, for years the real level of protection will continue its downward trend, unless nuclear opponents succeed in forcing a reconsideration of coverage. Is the existing level of coverage optimal, or would moving it higher or lower be appropriate?

Elegant models have been constructed that identify a unique level of coverage as an optimum (Cohen 1979; Wood 1982). The solution for this optimum, however, involves the value of unknown or unknowable parameters. At first glance, one can have a great deal of sympathy with the Supreme Court's opinion that any level of coverage would be arbitrary in nature. It turns out, though, that a rudimentary economic analysis can provide a useful framework for thinking about the problem and even rule out some solutions as dominated.

Consider the demand for nuclear insurance coverage and the cost of providing it. The demand for coverage lies in the benefit of reducing uncertainty about future levels of well-being for the potential victims of nuclear power plant accidents. A collective demand curve for dollars of coverage is easy to imagine as a total of the individuals' demand curves. Under usual assumptions, such a curve would shift rightward if there were an increase in the income of potential victims, the number of potential victims, or the amount of damage a nuclear accident could do.

The social cost of providing additional coverage is the expected value of accident damages (defined to include pain and suffering) plus any social risk premium. For small changes in wealth, an insurer holding a well-diversified portfolio of risks properly reckons the cost of offering insurance at just the expected value of the risk. There are some risks so big, however, that even the holder of a very large portfolio of risks—such as the goverment—sees the risk as more costly to insure than the simple expected value of the risk. For example, the expected value of a $100 billion risk that has a one in a billion chance of occurring per year is $100 per year. But recall that basing a premium on $100 per year for covering the risk means an accident occurring by chance within the first few hundred years would ruin the insurer. Surely the cost of insuring against such an accident includes a real premium for assuming the risk and is therefore greater than $100 per year.

One more aspect of insurance behavior is relevant here. A risk-averse person is one who would rather pay the expected value of a risk than face the risk without coverage, and it is usual to assume general risk aversion.[7] It follows that risk-averse individuals would insure themselves fully against accidents that could be covered for a cost equal to their expected loss. With insurance priced at more than its bare expected value, these individuals would choose something less than full coverage.

With only this rudimentary economic information in hand, policymakers could frame a more useful debate on the level of coverage for nuclear accidents than past debates. The appropriate level of coverage would occur where the marginal cost of providing another dollar of coverage is just equal to the collective marginal benefit of having the coverage provided. Placing the problem in such a framework would focus attention on the benefits of the coverage and the costs of providing it.

In particular, two propositions about appropriate coverage arrangements can be deduced. The first of these is that the original Price-Anderson framework was not internally consistent. Recall that the original government indemnity program provided $500 million in coverage for a fee designed to cover the government's administrative costs only: the costs of keeping the books, hiring secretaries, and the like. So low a fee was hardly an insurance premium at all, failing to include any compensation to the insurer for taking on such an extraordinary risk. However, if so low a fee really was appropriate—if it really cost so little to insure against this risk—then there would be no justification for providing less than full coverage. The original Price-Anderson framework sent conflicting signals.

One signal was that the risk was not very large, a signal sent by the extremely low fee charged for the government's insurance. The other signal was that the risk was very large indeed, a signal sent by the government's refusal to cover more than a small fraction of the potential damages.

This is not to say that full coverage is optimal. On the contrary, the cost of insuring completely against catastrophic nuclear risk is probably so high that full insurance against the maximum credible accident is not called for. The point is that such a low cost of coverage and less than complete coverage do not belong in the same legislative package. Either the high cost of insuring against catastrophe must be admitted, or full coverage would need to be provided. This is of more than historical interest, since some are now advocating that government provide $500 million more in coverage as under the old program (Alliance of American Insurers, nd).

Besides indicating that the original government indemnity program could not have been internally consistent, a simple economic model can provide some clues about how to change the level of coverage. The real level of protection provided by nuclear insurance has been declining, but the optimal level of coverage has been increasing. Consider the events of recent years, as interpreted through the collective demand curve for coverage. Population, income and reactor size (and so potential damages) have been increasing since the $560 million figure was set. These influences shift the marginal benefits farther upward than the marginal cost in a society of risk-averters. These influences would therefore call for a higher level of coverage, on the order of billions rather than millions. The only influence that would call for less coverage at the optimum would be a decreased probability of accidents. A decline in accident probabilities cannot be assumed with any confidence in view of the difficulties with the *Reactor Safety Study*. Thus the optimum level of coverage and the actual level have been moving in opposite directions since 1957.

RISKS OF ADOPTING A "MAGIC NUMBER"

This case study has shown how a particular number became enshrined in policymaking. The broad lessons for public policy may lie in what this case shows about the risks of embodying policy in a single number, especially when that single number is denominated in dollars. A single number expressed in dollars—whether it is nuclear insurance coverage or dollars per pupil in a school district or something else—will have a declining real value in the presence of inflation. That single number becomes part of the status quo, so that those who would change the number bear the burden of proof. In nuclear insurance, the inability of nuclear opponents to force a change in the $560 million figure has meant that the status quo is an ever-declining real level of protection. Prudence would seem to indicate at a minimum that the status quo be thought of as a constant real level of protection, meaning a level periodically adjusted for inflation. The level of nuclear liability coverage should be indexed for inflation, just as many homeowners' policies are.

Simple adjustment for inflation, however, does not end the risks to policymakers and institutions of embodying policy decisions in single numbers. Indeed, it may make the risks more subtle and hard to detect. If the insurance level for nuclear power were adjusted upward to account for inflation alone, policymakers and the industry might consider the task of adjustment complete. Yet adjusting for inflation alone would neglect some vital influences on the appropriate level of coverage—the growth of population around reactor sites and greatly increased size of reactors, to name two. Even an inflation-adjusted number is inflexible when real variables and real circumstances change.

A final danger of reliance on the single, "magic" number is that after many repetitions the number will tend to take on a life of its own. It may be repeated in contexts far removed from the context of its calculation, with the weaknesses and uncertainties in its origin gradually forgotten. To cite the $560 million level as having been set by "private insurance and government deliberations", is to invest it with an unwarranted credibility. Emphasis on the number itself can obscure the fact that the number was the sum of what private insurers were willing to risk more than 25 years ago, combined with an off-the-cuff guess about how much disruption the federal budget of the mid-1950s could withstand. Examples of emphasis on the bottom-line could be multiplied, but one more of special relevance will be cited. When the nuclear authorities were trying to specify the dollar harm of exposing a person to a "rem" of radiaton, they looked at the published range from previous risk-benefit analyses and adopted a round number of $1,000, slightly above the published high of $980. It seems precise to quote a damage figure of $1,000 as reflecting published technical work in radiation. But because of some odd twists in its derivation, it turns out—three sources removed from the policy decision—the figure is actually based on hazardous duty pay for Air Force pilots in 1962 (Wood 1983).

In summary, a single number embodying the policy can be inappropriate from the start or become inappropriate as conditions change. The risks to policymakers and institutions of adopting such numbers should not be underestimated.

CONCLUSIONS

A look at the record shows that policymakers deciding on a level of coverage for nuclear power plant accidents made little explicit use of the technical studies that were before them. Rather, they seized on a number which seemed an appropriate compromise between seeking to cover most accidents and not disturbing the public by suggesting the possibility of large accidents. In the face of the uncertainty surrounding the available technical advice and the inability to evaluate the technical evidence independently, legislators gladly accepted the round number that was concocted. In deciding on a figure, they had powerful incentives to come up with some solution that would not slow the development of nuclear power. They could be expected to proceed with some solution regardless of the outcome of any technical analysis.

The argument presented in this paper urges a focus on the demand for coverage and the cost of providing it. These are obvious elements to the thoughtful policy analyst but elements neglected so far in the search for an appropriate level of coverage. At the very least, policymakers should be aware of the dangers of embodying complex policy in a single unchanging number, and the importance of the signals they send by providing insurance at levels different from the optimum.

NOTES

1.   Some of the most important studies of nuclear power plant safety that are discussed in detail in the text are:

(AEC) U.S. Atomic Energy Commission. *Theoretical Possibilities and Consequences of Major Accidents at Large Nuclear Power Plants* (WASH-740). Washington: U.S. Atomic Energy Commission, March 1957.

(Interior) U.S. Congress. House Committee on Interior and Insular Affairs. Oversight & Investigations Subcommittee. "Calculation of Reactor Accident Consequences (CRAC2) for U.S. Nuclear Power Plants (Health Effects and Costs) Conditional on an 'SST1' Release," 97th Cong., 1st sess., November 1, 1982.

(NRC) U.S. Nuclear Regulatory Commission, *Reactor Safety Study: An Assessment of Accident Risks in U.S. Commercial Nuclear Power Plants* (NUREG-75/014). Washington: U.S. Nuclear Regulatory Commission, October 1975.

(WASH-740) "WASH-740 Update File." Available for copying and inspection at U.S. Nuclear Regulatory Commission Public Document Room, 1717 H Street, N.W., Washington, D.C. 20555.

(NUREG) Lewis, H.W., Chairman. *Risk Assessment Review Group Report to the U.S. Nuclear Regulatory Commission* (NUREG/CR-0400). Washington: U.S. Nuclear Regulatory Commission, September 1978.

2.   For a discussion of the verification problem, see the testimony of Chauncey Starr in the JCAE hearings (1974, 622).

3.   CAE means Joint Committee on Atomic Energy. This study is based on a series of JCAE hearings, noted in the text by year. Full citations follow:

U.S. Congress. Joint Committee on Atomic Energy. *Government Indemnity.* Hearings Before the Joint Committee on Atomic Energy, 84th Cong., 2d sess., 1956.

U.S. Congress. Joint Committee on Atomic Energy. *Government Indemnity and Reactor Safety.* Hearings Before the Joint Committee on Atomic Energy, 85th Cong., 1st sess., 1957.

U.S. Congress. Joint Committee on Atomic Energy. *H.R. 8631: To Amend and Extend the Price-Anderson Act.* Hearings Before the Joint Committee on Atomic Energy, 94th Cong., 1st sess., 1975.

U.S. Congress. Joint Committee on Atomic Energy. *Possible Modification or Extension* of the Price-Anderson Insurance and Indemnity Act. Hearings Before the Joint Committee on Atomic Energy, 93d Cong., 2d sess., 1974.

U.S. Congress. Joint Committee on Atomic Energy. Subcommittee on Legislation. *Proposed Extension of AEC Indemnity Legislation*. Hearings Before the Subcommittee on Legislation, 89th Cong., 1st sess., 1965.

4. P.L. 83-703, 42 USC 2012. For an excellent history of the period, see Green and Rosenthal (1963).

5. There was a discussion of unknown content off the record, however. See the JCAE hearings (1957, 45).

6. These results were never published, but they are available at the public document room of the Nuclear Regulatory Commission, 1717 H Street, N.W., Washington, D.C. 20555, as "WASH-740 Update File."

7. One argument for assuming risk aversion is that individuals and societies who do not insure against risks do not survive and prosper over the long run. For example, the agricultural society which does not store food but instead counts on a good harvest each year loses out over the long run to the society which provides for lean years. For further examples and other material in support of this point, see Sherman (1974, 92).

PART IV
NEW INSTITUTIONAL
ARRANGEMENTS

Chapter 7

THE INFLUENCE OF LEGISLATIVE MANDATES ON
THE OVERSIGHT OF RISK REGULATION AGENCIES
W. Kip Viscusi

Editor's Introduction

The new model we have proposed is partly descriptive, partly norma-
tive. If we no longer believe that risk analysis should be conducted in two
stages, we may be implying the need for new institutions that act according
to our new model. This section consists of three papers that, in widely
differing ways, consider whether and what kinds of new institutions we
might need. Viscusi's paper, the first of the three, could have been placed
in the first section, describing current conditions. I have placed it here
because, in describing the process of White House oversight of regulation,
Viscusi considers different oversight models. His description implicitly
posits a multi-stage model which is designed to achieve acceptable policy
decisions in the absence of complete scientific information.

The increased oversight of agency regulatory activities by the White
House has been perhaps the most striking development in governmental
risk control. Viscusi's paper describes an instance of this oversight exercised during the Carter administration, and contrasts it with developments
under Reagan, who strengthened the requirement that agencies provide
cost-benefit information on proposed regulatory activities and placed most
of the oversight power in the Office of Management and Budget. An
important question raised by these actions, which have been justified in
part as a means of obtaining more efficiency by allocating regulatory
dollars to the worst risks, is whether centralized management and comparison of risks can indeed yield a higher level of safety for the electorate.

So far, most of OMB's decisions seem to have resulted more from a mistrust of any regulation than from an effort to optimize the allocation of a ''safety budget.'' Centralized review does provide, however, a rare example of a new institution built in response to risk regulation; as Viscusi suggests, it is still in its shake-down period.

INTRODUCTION

Since November 1974, all proposed regulations imposing substantial costs have been subjected to systematic White House review. The chief elements of the review process during the Ford and Carter administrations included the preparation of an economic analysis of the regulation's likely effects (e.g., costs and comparison with regulatory alternatives) and public comment on these proposals by the White House staff. This review function was the responsibility of the Council on Wage and Price Stability (CWPS), which often worked in collaboration with the staff of the Office of Management and Budget and the Council of Economic Advisors.

The regulatory review staff was transferred to the Office of Management and Budget after Reagan abolished the Council on Wage and Price Stability in 1981. Reagan coupled this shift in organizational structure with an expansion of the authority of the oversight group. Instead of making non-binding public filings on proposed regulations, the oversight unit was given authority to require prior OMB approval of all proposed regulations. This authority was tantamount to veto power over regulations, although agencies do have appeals rights within this process.

Notwithstanding changes in administrations and organizational structure, the staff and substantive focus of the regulatory review process have remained fairly constant. From 1975–80 there was an average of about 50 regulatory analyses submitted annually by the Council on Wage and Price Stability, which are summarized in Table 1. Of these, approximately one-third were risk-related.

What is particularly striking is the falloff in regulatory activity for all agencies other than the Environmental Protection Agency (EPA) after 1978. This drop is attributable in part to the uncertainty posed by various court challenges to the Occupational Safety and Health Administration's (OSHA) legislative mandate, which would have broad ramifications across all risk regulations. The fundamental issue was whether agencies could focus exclusively on risk reduction and, most important, the extent to which cost-risk tradeoffs could enter into the policy design process. The risk regulation agencies maintained that their legislative mandates were absolute, requiring them to reduce risks irrespective of the cost. In these debates the regulatory agencies typically overstated the restrictiveness with which they actually regarded their legislative mandates. By claiming that their legislation imposed absolute requirements, agency officials were

Table 4

Council on Wage and Price Stability
Public Sector Releases Regarding Risk
Regulations, 1975−1980

Agency	1975	1976	1977	1978	1979	1980	Total
CPSC	1	3	1	− −	− −	− −	5
EPA	7	4	4	5	14	15	49
FDA	6	4	2	− −	1	1	14
NHTSA	4	1	2	1	− −	2	10
OSHA	2	4	5	2	− − −	1	14
Other Risk	1	2	− −	− −	− −	1	4
Total Risk	21	18	14	8	15	20	96
Total Filings	52	53	44	34	51	66	300
Rish Share of Total	.50	.34	.32	.24	.29	.30	.32

Source: W. Kip Viscusi, *Risk by Choice: Regulating Health and Safety in the Workplace* (Cambridge: Harvard University Press, 1983), 141.

primarily attempting to limit external interference with the tradeoffs that were in practice being made by the agency. For example, OSHA standards were based on an affordability criterion by which standards were not tightened to levels that were so stringent that the viability of the industry would be threatened. The participants in the White House oversight process maintained that while the legislation did not always *require* costs to be considered, the extent to which agencies *may* consider costs was not severely constrained.

The only agency that expanded its efforts in the presence of these uncertainties was the Environmental Protection Agency (EPA). EPA accounted for one-sixth of all CWPS reviews from 1975−80, but one-third of all reviews from 1979−80. The EPA risk regulation portion is even greater, as over three-fourths of all major risk regulations in the 1979−80 period were proposed by EPA.

The continued EPA activity was due in part to the more narrowly defined nature of EPA's risk reduction mandate. EPA was not given a vague mandate, but under the Clean Air Act was directed to provide an adequate margin of safety—a criterion EPA interpreted quite specifically. Moreover, EPA's legislation explicitly prohibited it from considering costs when setting ambient air quality standards.

EPA's actions during this period consequently may serve as a useful index of the kind of standards an agency will issue in situations in which its risk-based orientation is viewed as a legitimate basis for policy. In this paper I will analyze the design of the EPA lead standard to ascertain the role of these legislative requirements. The implications of this case will then be applied to assess likely trends at other agencies in view of the resolution of the controversial OSHA cases and the strengthened requirements of the regulatory oversight process.

In the following discussion, I will assume that the objective of regulatory policies should be to promote balanced policies that recognize the tradeoffs between risk and regulatory costs. More specifically, I will view the objective to be that of maximizing the net benefits (i.e., benefits less costs) to society.

The benefit-cost test is more stringent than a cost-effectiveness requirement whereby an agency would calculate the cost per unit risk averted and then promote a given level of risk reduction in the most efficient manner. In the Carter administration, the central oversight mechanism formally required that all new regulations be cost-effective, but this test was not enforced. The difference between cost-effectiveness analysis and benefit-cost analysis is that a benefit-cost test imposes a specific cost-effectiveness cutoff. For example, an agency may have structured its efforts so that it pursues the least costly means for preventing 10,000 cases of cancer, where the cost per case is $5 million. If society's willingness to pay for cancer reduction is only $1 million per case, this effort is not desirable on benefit-cost grounds. The agency should scale back its efforts, focusing on only the most effective cancer reduction policies that can achieve cancer reduction at a cost not in excess of $1 million.

Although basing policies on cost-effectiveness would be superior to present policy decisions, it is not ideal. In this paper I will use the benefit-cost framework primarily to provide an appropriate context for considering the issues that must be addressed in a sound regulatory analysis. Widespread implementation of the benefit-cost objective for risk regulation is by no means straightforward, particularly with regard to the estimation of health effects. Nevertheless, a benefit-cost approach is an instructive technique for tallying the pertinent effects of policies and for obtaining general guidance regarding the merits of a regulation. [1] Specific problems confronted when policymakers apply this criterion will be addressed later in the paper.

LEAD AND THE BENEFITS OF REGULATION

Lead emissions are a paradigmatic example of an economic externality since the market decision regarding the level of lead emissions will not reflect the adverse effects of lead on society in the absence of some emissions penalty or emissions standard (US EPA 1977). The chief source of lead emissions is antiknock additives in gasoline, which accounted for 12 times as many lead emissions as did all stationary sources in 1975. The role of auto emissions is expected to diminish due to the limits imposed on alkyl lead additives in gasoline. Nevertheless, the stationary sources that were the focus of the EPA lead standard will continue to contribute to only a small portion of an individual's lead exposure.

To address this problem, EPA established a lead standard of 1.5 micrograms per cubic meter of air (for simplicity, I will omit this metric in the discussion below, referring simply to an air lead level of 1.5). States were required to develop plans regulating stationary source emissions to meet this standard (43 *Federal Register* 46246 — 58, October 5, 1978).

Two features of this policy should be noted at the outset. First, the emissions standard was set uniformly for all states. If there is heterogeneity in either the incremental costs of compliance or the incremental benefits from lead exposure reduction, such a policy will not be optimal. The uniformity that should prevail is that the pollution standard for each state should equalize the incremental net benefits from further tightening of the standard. For example, other things being equal, a state with a large affected population should have a tighter standard, and states with an industry mix for which compliance is very costly should have a looser standard. The failure to reflect this heterogeneity stems from EPA's more general problem of focusing on risk reduction rather than a benefit-cost criterion, as will be discussed further below.

A second inadequacy of setting standards for stationary sources is that they constitute only a small portion of lead exposures. Although EPA correctly concluded that there was no major conflict among different lead regulation policies, such as the OSHA lead exposure standard and CPSC lead paint regulations, there was no attempt to analyze the most cost-effective policy mix. In the absence of such analysis, it is doubtful whether the independent selection of these policies will be the least expensive means for reducing air concentrations of lead. Since non-air sources of lead received even less consideration, the policymakers neglected a potentially effective means for affecting the fundamental matter of concern, which is the levels of lead concentration in human blood, not in the air.

Ideally, this problem of policy coordination should be an integral part of each agency's policy design efforts. There is little incentive to make such interagency comparisons since the legislative mandates do not prescribe that agencies pursue the most cost-effective mix. The White House regulatory oversight group could potentially fulfill such a role but, at least at the time of the EPA lead standard's promulgation, it did not have sufficient political influence to do so.

If it did have this authority, the White House oversight group could have examined the cost per unit health impact of different lead regulations—stationary sources, lead paint, and gasoline. It could then have ensured that the agencies' policies were cost-effective, i.e., the total benefits are provided in the least costly manner. Regulations that impose higher costs per case would be loosened, while those imposing lower costs per case would be tightened to result in equalizaton of the cost per health impact across agencies. Upon setting the absolute level of this cost-effectiveness ratio (e.g., a cost per case prevented of $X), the cost-effectiveness test becomes a benefit-cost criterion.

If we abstract from these broader issues and focus on the benefits from regulating stationary sources of lead emissions, the critical inputs needed to assess the benefits are the following: (1) the sources of lead emissions and their impact on airborne concentrations of lead; (2) the relation between air exposure levels and lead levels in the blood; (3) the health implications of these blood concentrations; and (4) the dollar value of these health effects.

The final category of considerations was ignored altogether. Although precise dollar equivalents for many health effects may be difficult to obtain, the relative severity of the health effects should have been analyzed. Moreover, even if the dollar value for different health impacts is unclear, it is usually instructive to make cost-effectiveness comparisons, indicating whether the cost per case of anemia prevented is $10,000 or $10 million.

EPA did address the first three considerations needed to assess benefits, although the information provided did not serve as a fully adequate basis for decision. The first issue—the source of airborne lead exposures—was addressed on an aggregative basis. It was noted, for example, that the lead standard would have its greatest effect on the operation of the metal products industries, such as primary smelting, secondary smelting, battery manufacturing, pigment manufacturing, and nonferrous foundries. However, information about the level of lead emissions in other areas is required in order to assess the benefits from reductions in these lead emissions adequately. Any regional variation in the implications of lead emissions will make it desirable to have different lead standards rather than a uniform national standard.

The second consideration—the effect of air exposure levels on blood lead levels—was treated by assuming that each microgram (per cubic meter) of air lead exposure increases the blood level by two micrograms (per deciliter of blood) for the group most affected by lead, young children. Although the accuracy of this rule of thumb is questionable, its role is limited to estimating the incremental effects of lead exposures. The actual blood lead level also depends on the level due to non-air sources as well, which EPA analyzed in some detail.

The greatest deficiency in the analysis is in the third and most fundamental category of concerns, the health implications of blood levels. A meaningful analysis of these health effects would assess the number of people with different lead-related ailments in the absence of regulation and the incremental effect on these health outcomes of different lead standards. In conjunction with information regarding the severity of the impacts and the costs of the different policies, the policy tradeoffs involved could be addressed directly.

EPA's neglect of these influences was not the result of an oversight or a failure to understand how to prepare a benefit-cost analysis. Rather, the difficulty was that EPA viewed its legislation as mandating a much narrower approach in which policies should not be based on their overall merits. The proper criterion was whether or not the standard provided an "adequate margin of safety." as directed by section 109 of the Clean Air Act. This mandate was interpreted to require that 99.5 percent of the most sensitive population be substantially below the threshold for adverse health effects. This criterion is based on a probability of safety that was selected arbitrarily by EPA, and it is independent of the number or severity of adverse health effects and totally independent of cost considerations. Quite simply, it has no economic justification whatsoever.

The shortcoming that I will focus on here is the use of health effect thresholds, since the threshold approach is quite common in risk analyses. Based on the limited medical evidence available, EPA concluded that the maximum safe blood lead level was 30 (micrograms per deciliter). At that level there is some evidence of impaired heme synthesis in cells, although the link to hemoglobin production or any other significant health impact is unclear. The lowest level at which there is a reasonably well-established link to a serious health effect is a blood level of 40, at which anemia is possible. More severe effects, such as brain damage, have been identified at blood levels from 80–100. EPA selected 30 as the critical threshold to provide a margin of safety. By the EPA's own analysis, there is no evidence of any adverse health effects between lead levels of 30 and 40. The arbitrary buffer level of 10 micrograms per deciliter yielded no expected risk reduction, but was a consequence of EPA's desire to provide a margin beyond a safe exposure level. Based on available evidence, it could be reasonably confident that this was a zero-risk level.

By setting standards at the highest level where studies have shown that there is no significant risk as opposed to the lowest level at which some risk has been identified, EPA goes beyond the approach of other risk regulation agencies that pursue reduction of identifiable risks. Although the neglect of cost-risk tradeoffs makes all of these risk-oriented approaches undesirable, EPA's policy is a more extreme variant of the absolutist approach to risk reduction.

Even if we abstract from the economic inefficiencies created by reducing lead exposure levels below the no-risk level, there is the additional problem that arises from making risk thresholds a central component in the analysis. The existence of a threshold only implies that there is some possible risk at that level. There is substantial debate within the medical profession as to whether threshold dose-response models are meaningful.

Other frameworks in which the risk is a continuous function of exposure, such as log-probit models or logistic models, often have superior statistical properties (Elandt-Johnson and Johnson 1980). Even when a threshold model is appropriate, the existence of a threshold only identifies the exposure level at which the risk is not zero. In the usual case, it is assumed that the risk is zero just below the threshold, is just above zero at the threshold, and increases linearly with exposure levels above the threshold. The probability of the adverse outcome typically does not jump from zero to one simply because the threshold has been reached. In the case of the EPA lead standard, the regulatory cost that can be justified will be quite different if the health risk at the threshold is .1 or .0001.

The net effect of the EPA approach is to ensure that only 0.5 percent of the most sensitive segment of the population would have blood lead levels well below a level associated with any adverse effects. Moreover, even the risk threshold level of 40 is relatively safe, since more serious effects such as anemia do not occur until lead levels ten micrograms higher.

This policy was formulated independent of the number of adverse health effects prevented, the severity of these effects, and the costs imposed on society. Such an approach can only be justified if one places an infinite value on even minor health effects, which is a rather tenuous basis for policy.

THE COSTS OF THE EPA LEAD STANDARD

The most beneficial consequence of the White House regulatory review process is that agencies now calculate the projected costs of significant new regulations. EPA calculated these costs to comply with the oversight guidelines, but it did not include cost considerations in the policy design since doing so would have violated the requirements of the Clean Air Act.

The proposed lead standard, which was based on monthly exposure levels of 1.5, entailed capital investment costs of $620 million and annualized costs of $137 million.[2] The variation in the impact by industry is considerable, with two-thirds of the burden being on two industries—primary copper smelting and grey iron foundry casting—and almost all of the remainder borne by three industries—primary lead smelting, secondary lead smelting and the lead-acid battery industry.

The relative impact of these costs also varied substantially, as the lead standard would require capital investments almost five times greater than the current level of capital expenditures in the primary copper smelting industryand the grey iron foundry casting industries, and considerably smaller effects on other industries.

The differential burdens imposed on these industries suggest that there is also likely to be wide variation in the incremental costs of lead emission reduction across different industries. Since within any particular area the benefits of lead exposure reduction depend on the level in the air, not on which source has been affected, the most cost-effective way to reduce lead exposures is to vary the emissions standard across industries to equalize the incremental costs of lead emissions reductions.

This type of calculation is not possible with the data available since the focus of EPA's cost estimates was on the overall cost for the economy rather than on the variation of these costs with different standards. As with the benefit information discussed earlier, EPA did not generate the type of information needed to make an informed policy choice since their own policy objectives emphasized risk reduction rather than benefit-cost tradeoffs, and the requirements imposed by the regulatory review process were not sufficient to redirect EPA's efforts as fully as needed.

It is generally agreed that the impact of the regulatory review process on risk regulations in the 1970s was, at best, relatively modest. To some extent, the failure to reform risk regulation was attributable to the absence of more effective political power for the regulatory review agency. But even if the influence of the regulatory oversight group had been strengthened, optimal decisions would not have resulted without a change in the substantive focus of the agency's regulatory analyses. As the EPA lead case indicates, the information needed to make these choices was never provided.

Ideally, one would like to have perfect information about the implications of policies so that the policy choice can be based on the relative merits of the available alternatives. Unfortunately, some key ingredients of the analysis, such as the nature of the dose-response relationships, are not well known. In these cases, policymakers should explore the implications of different assumptions about the nature of these relationships; the present approach to decisions can only be justified if one assumes that the risk jumps from zero to one once a critical threshold is reached.

Many presently omitted components of the analysis are excluded because of the EPA's narrowly construed policy objective rather than because of the absence of the necessary informaton. Regional variations in the benefits of a regulation hinge primarily on the size and composition of the exposed population. Similarly, the heterogeneity in the costs imposed by a regulation also depends on usually well known parameters, such as the region's industry mix and the difference in the costs of compliance by industry (Viscusi 1983).

Establishment of a sound basis for regulation will promote the better utilization of currently available information and will enable policymakers to make more precise judgments on the sensitivity of the optimal policy choice to the values of parameters that are not known. Moreover, since the information provided by agency staff and by contractors to the agency is usually linked to the agency's policy objectives, the provision of pertinent information should be enhanced by the use of better criteria for selecting policies. Whether or not such information will be provided depends both on the judicial interpretation of a risk-based legislative mandate and the regulatory oversight requirements. These matters are the focus of the remainder of the paper.

THE OSHA COURT CASES

The types of inadequacies affecting the EPA lead policy were not restricted to policies under the Clean Air Act but exemplified the general kinds of distortions generated by a narrowly defined risk orientation. Other agencies also had relatively myopic concerns, but uncertainties raised by the OSHA court tests made these risk reduction mandates less pronounced and brought new rulemaking activity by risk regulation agencies almost to a standstill during the second half of the Carter Administration.

The judicial uncertainties were resolved by the 1980 benzene decision and the 1981 cotton dust decision by the U.S. Supreme Court.[3] In the benzene case, the court overturned the OSHA standard on the grounds that OSHA had not shown that the hazard was a ''significant risk.'' What the court meant by significant risk is unclear. While the focus was apparently on the probability of the adverse outcome, presumably the severity of the outcome and the number of people affected also affect judgments regarding significance. If all of these factors are permitted to enter, then the significant risk concept becomes tantamount to a benefit calculation. The benefits of risk reduction are simply the product of the change in the risk probability, the number of people affected, and weights for the severity of the health effects, where these weights are based on the beneficiaries' willingness to pay for the risk reduction.

Whereas the benzene case appeared to limit the discretion of risk regulation agencies, the cotton dust decision pointed in the opposite direction. OSHA was explicitly prohibited from using a benefit-cost criterion to set standards for ''toxic substances and harmful physical agents,'' such as cotton dust. Instead, reduction of significant risks was to be undertaken to the extent feasible, where feasibility was given the narrow interpretation of ''capable of being done.''

Although intended to resolve the confusion regarding legislative mandates, the cotton dust case was not conclusive. The original cotton dust standard was set on the basis of a cost-effectiveness criterion, whereby the stringency of the standard was varied according to the stage of processing (Viscusi 1983, Chapter 7). OSHA in effect established an arbitrary cost-risk tradeoff not linked to a specific benefit level; it did not attempt to suppress cost considerations or to focus only on technical feasibility, which is the concept upheld by the court.

More fundamentally, there is no way to assess technical feasibility independent of cost considerations. At one extreme, feasibility might be viewed in terms of the technical possibility of compliance if one were willing to commit sufficient funds, however great. Such an interpretation would lead to unduly burdensome regulations, and in practice cost considerations and cost-risk tradeoffs will enter, though perhaps not explicitly.

The net effect of these court cases is to uphold a risk-based orientation but to make regulators focus only on significant risks, an approach which presumably embodies many benefit considerations, and to emphasize technical feasibility, which intrinsically involves cost considerations. Moreover, cost-effectiveness tests, such as those used in setting the cotton dust standard, have not been ruled out.

In the case of independent agencies, the effect of these decisions has been to give independent agencies relatively free reign. The 1981 shift of the regulatory oversight functions to OMB sacrificed the authority of CWPS to intervene in rulemaking proceedings of independent agencies so that these agencies are constrained only by their legislative mandates, judicial review, and possible congressional action. If the agencies interpret these mandates narrowly, focusing on risk considerations alone, the result will be a continuation of the narrow risk-based policies of the past.

Unlike OSHA, which addresses significant risks, the Consumer Product Safety Commission (CSPC) focuses on "unreasonable risks." The level of risk qualifying as unreasonable has never been defined. In practice, the CPSC has focused on total injuries rather than the risk level on a use-adjusted frequency basis (Viscusi, forthcoming). In most cases it is the total number of product accidents that has dictated policy interventions because of the agency's focus on total injuries rather than market failures. This has led to the regulation of comparatively safe products posing annual death risks of 1 in 100,000 or less. The risk-based criterion provides little effective constraint on policies. Since CPSC has explicitly disavowed the use of a benefit-cost test, the potential for misguided policies is great.

The situation at the Nuclear Regulatory Commission (NRC) is similar since NRC has recently determined that its safety criterion is whether or not nuclear plants pose "significant additional risk." More specifically, NRC has proposed that the risk of instant death or lethal cancer from nuclear accidents for all persons should not exceed 1/1000 of their overall risk from other causes.

Such arbitrary risk-based criteria certainly do not provide a sound basis for policy. What matters is whether the benefits of risk reduction (including the *number* of people affected) are commensurate with the costs. At the very minimum, the agency should adopt a cost-effectiveness approach whereby it calculates the cost per case of cancer prevented and then adopts the policies that will control these nuclear risks at the least expense. Tighter regulations or weaker regulations may emerge using a benefit-cost tradeoff, depending on the particular circumstances. What is clear is that arbitrary selected risk cutoff levels do not provide a sound basis for policy.

THE REGULATORY OVERSIGHT PROCESS

The implications of the OSHA decisions for executive branch agencies are less sharply defined. The Reagan Administration strengthened the oversight process, imposing a benefit-cost test except when doing so was ruled out by the agency's legislative mandate. Since OSHA cannot base policies on such a test, for that agency the new rules have had limited applicability. Similarly, the Food and Drug Administration bases its drug regulations on the existence of a "substantial risk," and the Delaney Amendment requires FDA to reduce food cancer risks to zero. The National Highway Traffic Safety Administration (NHTSA) has also resisted OMB, as it refuses to even do cost-effectiveness (i.e., cost per life saved) calculations for its regulations, much less to act on the implications of such analyses. EPA has remained in roughly the same position as was illustrated in the lead standard case.

While benefit-cost tests cannot be formally imposed, OMB has been successful in making agencies provide the kind of information needed to make such a determination. In most instances, benefits and costs are both calculated quite explicitly, although the agencies will not explicitly compare these magnitudes when a benefit-cost test is prohibited.

If agencies had the same discretion they possessed under the previous administratons, these additional informational inputs would be of little consequence. Agencies would continue to issue policies based on narrow risk-based concerns. In the past, the White House oversight group could potentially have halted these policies, but doing so required Presidential intervention. In the major CWPS cases in which the controversy was elevated to that level—the OSHA cotton dust standard and the EPA "superfund" policy—the decision was in favor of the regulatory agencies so that this appeals process made little difference during the Carter Administration.

The balance of power is quite different under the present oversight system. Before proposing a regulation, agencies need prior approval by OMB. In practice, OMB examines the regulatory analyses in detail and is able to impose very stringent criteria on new regulatons. There is no practical barrier to applying a benefit-cost test. Agencies are required to provide the information needed for such a judgment, and OMB need not publicly state the reasons for its decisions to halt or approve regulatory initiatives.

Agencies could potentially appeal OMB vetos of regulatory proposals to the Vice-President's regulatory task force. Since the executive director of this task force is also the head of the OMB oversight group, however, the staff support for the appeals process will be provided by the same OMB staff that rejected the original proposal, creating a strong presumption in favor of OMB and against the agency.

It is noteworthy that notwithstanding the restrictive legislative mandates of the risk regulation agencies, the first case appealed to the Vice-President focused on benefit-cost issues. In 1982, OMB refused to allow OSHA to propose its hazard communications standard because the risk reduction assumptions were overly optimistic so that the costs were far in excess of the benefits. OSHA appealed OMB's action, focusing on the merits of the OMB arguments rather than on the obligations created by the Occupational Safety and Health Act. Vice-President Bush likewise did not focus on the legal obligations, but requested that the agencies settle the substantive differences in the analyses before making his decision.

I was asked by OMB and the Department of Labor to prepare an unbiased assessment of this conflict. Although almost all of OMB's substantive objections were correct, OSHA's failure to value the health benefits properly led to a significant understatement of benefits. In particular, measures of individual willingness to pay for risk reduction exceeded OSHA's earnings loss estimates by a factor of 10. Shortly after the White House received my analyis supporting the desirability of the regulation on benefit-cost grounds Vice-President Bush overruled OMB and permitted OSHA to propose the regulation.[4]

What is most striking is not the policy outcome but the fact that benefit-cost concerns dominated the policy debate. In the Carter Administration, the White House oversight group occasionally raised such issues, but it seldom pursued them since the regulatory agency officials were not receptive to such an approach. Most suggested regulatory reforms were intended to eliminate gross inefficiencies rather than to obtain an ideal policy outcome.

If OMB continues to use a benefit-cost test, the policies that emerge will be much sounder than before. However, there is no assurance that this will be the case, and with no public accountability there is no means of ascertaining the basis of OMB's actions.

The impetus for OMB decisions may stem in part from the internal structure of the oversight group. The policy analysis staff, which consists of the former CWPS regulatory group, focuses on benefit-cost issues, while the much larger paperwork staff is concerned with the regulatory burden per se. If the paperwork staff's influence dominates, the results will be regulatory decisions based primarily on costs rather than benefit-cost tradeoffs. It is doubtful whether cost-based policy choices will be much better than the risk-based policies on the past.

The potential for abuse has become apparent in the Department of Transportation's decision to halt NHTSA's passive restraint standard for autos. Although the decision may have been correct, the justification for postponing the regulation was not compelling. The Department of Transportation based its decision on what it viewed to be ambiguities in the evidence regarding the effectiveness of passive restraints. Similar ambiguities in the benefit estimates pertain to virtually all risk regulation efforts. If regulations are rejected whenever benefits are controversial and cost estimates are precise, a strong bias against regulations, many of which may be good, will emerge. The policy criterion should be the expected benefits less costs, based on the best evidence available, even if it is imprecise. Whereas policies previously were based on risk considerations alone, there is the danger that cost considerations have now become dominant. Neither partial approach is an effective means for promoting sound risk regulation policies.

Although it is too soon to tell whether such a policy shift has occurred, OMB has already exhibited a tendency to rely on the inherent ambiguity of the scientific evidence to serve as a justification for its policy decisions. In the case of the OSHA hazard communication standard, for example, the lack of any precise estimate of the share of cancer cases arising from occupational exposures was the major substantive concern expressed by OMB. For proposals under earlier administrations, such as the EPA lead standard, agencies used the ambiguity regarding the magnitude of the dose-response relationship to justify very stringent policies tied to the lowest exposure level at which some risk was possible. The purported justification for these actions was the legislative requirement to provide a ''margin of safety'' or some similar guarantee of safety. OMB can now rely on this same ambiguity to argue that agencies have failed to show that standards will result in a significant reduction in risk. OMB may adopt this approach publicly but in practice may base its policy decisions on benefit-cost judgments, cost considerations, or some other criterion. Although such tests cannot be formally used in the wake of the cotton dust case, there is no practical limit to OMB's discretion.

The somewhat muddled scientific basis for risk regulations consequently creates substantial political maneuverability for making regulatory decisions on the basis of transient political judgments rather than the long-term interests of society. So long as the informational inputs to benefit-cost analyses remain imprecise, this discretion will remain. Although most recent attempts to reform the regulatory process have focused on the economic criteria for policy design and evaluation, equally important is the underlying scientific basis for these policies.

CONCLUSION

Meaningful regulatory reform requires three kinds of changes. First, the risk-based legislative mandates of the regulatory agencies should be replaced with an explicit benefit-cost test or, at the very minimum, elimination of legislative requirements that prohibit such tests. This change will enable policymakers to make the kinds of tradeoffs needed so that balanced policies will emerge in the agencies' policy design process. Second, Congress should give OMB the authority to make public its regulatory positions by returning to the oversight group the public filing authority the CWPS group had under Ford and Carter. OMB also should be required to make public the reasons for its regulatory decisions and to document these decisions with the same thoroughness that CWPS did in the past.

Despite OMB's public commitment to benefit-cost analysis, this criterion for decision does not ensure optimal decisions. Particularly for risk regulation policies, there is often a wide divergence in estimates of the benefits of the regulation. Benefit-cost analyses can best serve to define the nature of the policy debate rather than resolve all policy controversies. Cost-effectiveness analysis can serve a similar role, although ultimately policymakers must select a cost per risk reduction cutoff, at which time this criterion becomes tantamount to a benefit-cost test. The extent to which the function of policy analysis will be constructive depends in part on the quality of the scientific evidence underlying the regulation. The present scientific ambiguities serve to limit the usefulness of economic analyses which can be more readily manipulated when the underlying technical information is imprecise. Even with imprecise evidence one can make sounder regulatory decisions than have been made in the past by using the limited evidence available to promote more balanced approaches to risk regulation.

NOTES

1. For further discussion of the valuation of health effects and related policy issues, see Viscusi (1983).

2. These estimates are based on EPA's *Background Support Document for Economic Impact Assessment of the Lead Ambient Air Quality Standard* (January, 1979). These cost estimates were analyzed in some detail within the White House oversight unit in the insightful internal memorandum by Thomas Hopkins and Dianne Levine.

3. The 1980 benzene case is the U.S. Supreme Court Decision in the Case of AFL-CIO Industrial Union Dept. v. American Petroleum Institute, et. al., and the 1981 cotton dust case is the Decision in the Case of American Textile Manufacturers Institute et.al. v. Donovan, Secretary of Labor.

4. My analysis is contained in W. Kip Viscusi, "Analysis of OMB and OSHA Evaluations of the Hazard Communication Proposal," report submitted to Secretary of Labor Raymond Donovan, March 15, 1982. See the *New York Times,* March 23, p. 13 (national edition) for discussion of the influence of this report on the policy outcome.

Chapter 8

INSTITUTIONAL MECHANISMS FOR RESOLVING RISK CONTROVERSIES [1]
Mark Rushefsky

Editor's Introduction

Rushefsky's article explicitly considers two new decision-making procedures that have been tried only in limited ways: science panels and
regulatory negotiation. Science panels are especially interesting in the
context of this book since they are designed expressly to perfect the
two-stage model by improving the scientific analysis of the first stage.
Regulatory negotiation, on the other hand, embodies an assumption that
policy is made by a more complex, iterative process such as the one
proposed in the introduction. There are advantages and disadvantages of
both new processes. How serious the disadvantages are depends on a
variety of conditions that Rushefsky describes. Although regulatory
negotiation will require greater creativity of institution builders, it also
seems to me to be more flexible precisely because it is based in the iterative
rather than in the two-stage model.

INTRODUCTION

As science and technology have developed, perspectives on that development have changed from awe over the benefits to concern about
potential harm. That concern, expressed politically by the environmental
and consumer movements, has been translated into a vast outpouring of
legislation, especially at the federal level, directly or indirectly designed to

133

antitipate, control and limit potential impacts of technological development. Table 5 displays this growth in federal legislation.

Table 5

Federal Health, Safety, and Environmental Legislation in Effect

Year

Year	
1900	xx
1950	xxxx
1955	xxxxx
1960	xxxxxxxx
1965	xxxxxxxx
1970	xxxxxxxxxxxxxx
1975	xxxxxxxxxxxxxxxxxxxxxxxxxx
1980	xxxxxxxxxxxxxxxxxxxxxxxxxxxxxxxx

Note: each 'x' equals one law currently in effect

Source: Dodge and Civiak 1981

Risk management is the process of anticipating and controlling hazards due to technological development. Most risk management is conducted by the private sector, for example, in the development of product standards. Increasingly, risk management activities are being conducted by the public sector and numerous agencies have risk management responsibilities: i.e., the Environmental Protection Agency (EPA), the Consumer Products Safety Commission (CPSC), the Food and Drug Administration (FDA), and the Occupational Safety and Health Administraton (OSHA).

For the reasons discussed in the introduction to this volume, the legislation and its implementation have been extremely controversial, with battles fought over policy priorities, allocation of resources and regulatory standards (Crowfoot 1980). Industrial interests have complained of burdensome regulations and "overraction" to perceived hazards. Environmental and consumer interests have complained about the slow pace of implementation and the inadequacy of laws and regulations. The Reagan Administration designated many risk management regulations as candidates for regulatory reform and the Senate passed, in 1981, a comprehensive regulatory reform bill (S. 1080) designed to stem the flow of regulations and tighten legislative and judicial oversight. President Reagan's Executive Order #12291, expanding an earlier executive order by President Carter (#12044), calls for cost-benefit analysis of proposed regulations with oversight by the Office of Management and Budget

(OMB). The Senate bill also called for regulatory analysis but limited OMB's authority.

Thus, health and safety regulation is an important current political issue, forming the backdrop of the Reagan Administration's promise for regulatory relief. A major policy question is the form this relief will take. The possibilities are numerous. The administration can attempt to reduce the volume of regulation,[2] or encourage more efficient, cost effective regulations based on cost-benefit analysis. An intriguing set of alternatives, similar to economic deregulation, includes private self-regulation and compensatory remedies, modified by government influence (i.e., government procurement and information policies and notices of intent to regulate) (Baram 1982). The assumption of this chapter is that traditional regulation will remain the predominant mode of managing risks by government. The problem then is how to create structures and processes that will simultaneously reduce conflict and the impact of conflict on governmental processes and legitimacy while producing scientifically sound decisions acceptable to interested parties. The remainder of the chapter will first discuss the risk management process and criticisms of that process and then evaluate two institutional proposals addressing those criticisms, centralized science panels and regulatory negotiation.

RISK MANAGEMENT IN THE REGULATORY PROCESS

The Risk Management Process

There have been several attempts to characterize the risk management process; two formulations are presented in Table 6. Both divide risk management into two phases: technical determinations and policy decisions. Technical determination, the objective or factual portion of the process, is conducted by government and outside (i.e., industry) experts, with reviews by appropriate agencies. Based on this, agencies make decisions about whether and to what extent exposure to a hazard is acceptable; this second phase is the value or subjective portion of the process.

Criticisms of Risk Assesment

Critics have attacked both the scientific and political elements of the risk management process. For example, questions are raised concerning the adequacy of the scientific evidence, the various methodologies employed (i.e., animal experiments, epidemiological studies), and the validity of extrapolation from those studies to human exposure (Office of Technology Assessment 1981).

Table 6

Steps in the Risk Management Process

Tobin/Lowrance	National Research Council
Technical Determinations	

1. impact of a technology
  a. conditions of exposure
  b. nature of hazard
  c. relationship of exposure to effect
  d. estimate of risk
	1. hazard identification
	2. dose response assessment
	3. exposure assessment
	4. risk characterization

Political Determinations	
2. government reviews data and assesses risk	5. analysis of regulatory options
3. government determines risk acceptability	6. agency decisions

Sources: Tobin 1979; Lowrance 1976; National Research Council 1982

The validity of the animal tests themselves has also been disputed. A recent article by Salsburg and Heath (1981) suggests that animal studies have overestimated the extent to which chemicals cause cancer. They argue that the National Cancer Institute's assumptions about testing no longer correspond to new knowledge about "cancer paths," that some chemicals reduce the risk of certain cancers, and that we should test for all kinds of health problems, not just carcinogens. What is needed, they conclude, are "new scientific and philosophical framework(s)." However, the bureaucracy has been slow to acknowledge the changes let alone act upon them (Salsburg and Heath 1981, 38). In addition, apparently a considerable number of laboratory animal studies were conducted under fraudulent conditions and relied upon as an important factor in many risk decisions. Fraudulent research compounds the regulatory controversy by questioning the scientific validity of risk decision, but in a different direction from the Salsburg and Heath critique (Dowie et al. 1982; Rushefsky, in progress).

One frequently mentioned political criticism is the inconsistency of the various statutes. Some are zero-risk laws, effectively permitting no exposure to a substance regardless of cost or feasibility. Others are balancing laws, which weigh health risks against other factors such as cost, economic impact, and availability of substitutes. A third type of legislation is technology-based, requiring either the meeting of standards for which the technology has yet to be developed (technology-forcing) or the use of best available technology (Office of Technology Assessment 1981; Regens, Dietz, and Rycroft 1983).

A second political complaint about public sector risk management is the overlap of various mandates. For example, vinyl chloride comes under the jurisdiction of the four major regulatory agencies (EPA, CPSC, OSHA and FDA) plus numerous statutes (Doniger 1978). While a case can be made for redundancy (Landau 1969; Anthony 1982), overlap has created problems of coordination, which lead the Carter administration to form an Interagency Liaison Regulatory Group (IRLG) composed of representatives of those four agencies.

A third political problem is the cumbersomeness and length of risk management procedures. Government decision-making can take years, involve numerous steps, and still not resolve the specific issue. For example, the Department of Agriculture began investigating the herbicide 2,4,5-T in 1970. Later, as pesticide regulation was shifted to the Environmental Protection Agency, that agency also considered action to limit the use of the herbicide in the early 1970s, only to withdraw proposed actions. In 1978, EPA began the rebuttable presumption against registration (RPAR) process against 2,4,5-T and in 1979 issued an emergency suspension of most of the herbicide's uses. The two actions (RPAR and the suspension) were consolidated into one administrative hearing which consumed some 28,000 pages of transcript. In 1981, the hearings were suspended and EPA and industry began informal negotiations. After some twelve years of discussion and stop-and-start regulatory proceedings, the 2,4,5-T issue remains to be resolved (Rushefsky 1982).

Finally, there are criticisms that combine the political and scientific aspects. A number of opponents of regulation (e.g., Wolf 1979) see government as "risk averse." The tendency of governmental agencies to avoid blame has been explained by Anthony (1982). He suggests that risk control institutions that are charged with the goal "do not fail" must respond to this open-ended mandate by continued elaboration of their backups. Thus, regulatory agencies employ conservative risk assumptions to avoid blame in the event of a mistake or catastrophe, such as Love Canal or Times Beach. This is discussed at length by the American Industrial Health Council (AIHC) in its analysis of the Interagency Regulatory Liaison Group (IRLG) report on risk assessment:

> When the IRLG Report speaks of the importance of using conservative methods or assumptions so as not to underestimate human risk, the Report is mixing regulatory considerations into

> the scientific function. The scientific determination should be made separately from the regulatory determinations. On the basis of the best scientific estimate of the real risk, the regulatory agency can then consider costs, benefits, and other elements that enter into a regulatory determination. Those regulatory considerations should not be injected into the scientific function in some undisclosed way. Science is neither conservative nor non-conservative. The objective of the scientific analysis should be to provide, as to the OSTP Report points out, the risk estimate that has the greatest probability of being accurate and to provide a measure of the confidence limits thereof (American Industrial Health Council 1979, I-6).

The great dissatisfaction with the current process of risk management is also evident in numerous court cases involving agency action and inaction such as the cotton dust (*American Textile Manufacturers Institute* v. *Donovan*) and benzene (*American Petroleum Institute* v. *Marshall*) cases, discussed by Vig (this volume). This general criticism from all sides weakens the legitimacy of government. The thrust of many of these criticisms is that the scientific elements cannot really be separated from the political elements, though the intent of some may be precisely to make that separation. Regulatory solutions must address both aspects simultaneously, especially when (as is generally the case) full scientific information is not available. Thus, one criterion for evaluating proposed solutions is the extent to which they recognize this inevitable intermingling of facts and values.

PROPOSED SOLUTIONS

Conceptually, as we have seen, risk management has been divided into two major components: technical assessment of risks posed by a technology; and the political decision as to whether and to what extent to limit the technology. The institutional proposals similarly divide along these two dimensions: centralized science panels for technical determinations; and regulatory negotiations for policy decisions.

Both sets of proposals have attained the institutional agenda (Cobb and Elder 1972), though action by Congress is not imminent in 1983. The earliest science panel proposals were for a science court (Kantrowitz 1976; Matheny and Williams 1981; Task Force 1976), but were never implemented.

Centralized science panels were the subject of two pieces of legislation in 1981, H.R. 638 (The National Science Council Act) and H.R. 3441 (The Risk Analysis Research and Demonstration Act). Proposals for such centralized bodies have been recommended by the American Industrial Health Council (1980), Judge Howard T. Markey (U.S. in Congress, Joint Hearings 1980) and the Office of Science and Technology Policy (OSTP), Executive Office of the White House (Calkins et al. 1980). In addition, Congress mandated a study of the feasibility of centralized science panels, which was completed in early 1983 (National Research Council 1982, 1983; see also Office of Technology Assessment, 1981). The National Research Council report calls for a Central Board on ''Risk Assessment Methods'' (National Research Council 1983) and William Ruckelshaus, administrator of the Environmental Protection Agency, recommended a national commission to measure health risk and willingness to pay to reduce risk.[3]

Whether or not science panels can reduce conflict and produce better, or at least more acceptable, decisions is an extremely important question. In one respect, opponents of the plans question the validity of the basic assumptions of science panels, that science and policy, facts and values, can be separated. One study suggests that such distinctions are difficult to maintain in reality because of epistemological differences among scientists (Rushefsky 1982). Even if a science panel were employed, conflict reduction might not follow. One of the basic problems of science and technology disputes is that resolution is difficult and alternative interpretations are possible precisely because scientific information is not definitive (Mazur 1973; Weinberg 1972). For these two reasons alone, science panels by themselves are unlikely to solve many of the problems discussed in the first part of the chapter. An alternative or complementary institutional mechanism is necessary: regulatory negotiation.

Regulatory negotiation is a generic name for a whole series of processes that explicitly seek to resolve political controversies. The concept is based on the literature of conflict resolution and includes various forms of mediation between the parties to a dispute with the object of producing decisions or agreements acceptable to all parties or at least understanding of the positions held by different parties. Negotiation can be categorized into three basic types. One type occurs when an intervenor acts on national policy issues; this type is what is referred to in this chapter as regulatory negotiation. A second type occurs in site specific dispute. And a third type is a consensual framework—a collaborative problem solving model, for example in facilitating meetings.[4]

The rationale for mediation is that under the present system disputants rarely meet face to face; rather, disputants address agencies or courts, rendering dialogue difficult. Because of the adversarial nature of regulatory and judicial processes, each side attempts to present its position in the best light and its opponents' positions in the worst; this leads to polarization of positions. Finally, several commentators have noted that the disputants are unhappy with the outcomes of regulatory and judicial processes and thus have a stake in producing more acceptable results (Harter 1982;

Susskind and Weinstein 1980).

As with centralized science panels, regulatory negotiation has also been the subject of government activity. Hearings on the idea have been held (Select Committee, 1980); three bills were proposed in 1981 (H.R. 1336, The Regulatory Negotiation Commissions Act; S. 1360, The Regulatory Negotiation Act; and S. 1601, The Regulatory Mediation Act); the concept has been recognized and praised by the Reagan administration;[5] and the Administrative Conference of the United States has recommended that federal agencies consider the process (47 Federal Register 30708, July 15, 1982). In response, the Environmental Protection Agency began a regulatory negotiation project in 1983 (Environmental Protection Agency 1983), with other agencies to follow, including the Department of Transportation.

To explore and evaluate further these two sets of institutional proposals, a comparison will be made following the outlines of Tables 7 and 8.

Table 7

Science Panels

Purpose: to improve the evaluation of scientific evidence used in making risk decisions

Theoretical Basis: technocratic

Structure: centralized board that would make risk assessments

Participants: eminent scientists, technical experts, comprising the board plus the use of advisory committees

Outcome: a quantitative and qualitative risk assessment that would be a major input into risk decision-making

Assumptions:
1. risk management decisions have been based on poor scientific evidence
2. separation of technical (fact) and political (value) elements of risk decisions is not only feasible but vital to good decision-making
3. technical experts can resolve many of the controversial technical disagreements
4. science panels can limit the range of disagreements to political rather than technical areas

Table 8

Regulatory Negotiation

Purpose: to reduce the amount of controversy over risk decisions by producing agreement among interested parties

Theoretical Basis: corporatist

Structure: negotiating groups set up on an ad hoc basis, employing the "rule of reason"

Participants: convenor, mediator, representatives of interest groups

Outcome: a recommendation to an agency based on group consensus

Assumptions:
1. all parties in risk controversies are unhappy with present outcomes
2. the use of technical expertise will not diffuse political controversies
3. the present structure of risk decision-making polarizes the disputants
4. there are many areas of agreement among various affected interests
5. dialogue produces greater understanding among affected parties

Purpose

The overall purpose of centralized science panels and regulatory negotiation is to improve public sector decision making concerning exposure to various technological hazards. Within this overall purpose, the two proposals differ according to their place in the risk management process.

Science panels speak to the technical component of risk management. Their purpose is to improve the evaluation of scientific evidence used in making risk decisions. Many of the criticisms discussed earlier relate to the quality of the science used. Those advocating science panels believe that poor science, weak methodologies, and inadequate reviews lead to questionable regulatory decisions. Thus, the panel proposals seek to improve agency decisions by rewarding good science and enhancing the basis for agency determinations.

Regulatory negotiation, on the other hand, seeks a different result. Its purpose is to reduce political controversy (as is the implicit goal of science panels) by producing agreement among affected parties in a particular dispute. In one sense, regulatory negotiation has a rather long history. An agency, such as the Consumer Product Safety Commission, will work with affected industry to adopt voluntary standards as an alternative to issuing regulations. Such procedures reduce the amount of direct government intervention and the conflicts that often surround such actions.

While agencies do have this experience with negotations, a more formal regulatory negotiationprocess is needed for two reasons. First, the voluntary standards process involves only industry groups, whereas environmental, health, and safety regulations often are of concern to other interests (e.g., labor, environmental, and consumer groups) that may lack the experience and resources needed to ensure wider participation. Second, what has been called the "hot tub" theory may not be appropriate for all rules. "People do not get together to resolve a dispute with beguiling openness and reasonableness simply because the process has been labelled non-adversarial. Rather, a party needs an incentive to negotiate by believing it will be better off for having done so" (Harter 1982, 45). The incentive to involve nonindustry interests is the ability of those interests to successfully challenge rules, guidelines, and standards. Regulatory negotiation, again, is one method to reduce political conflict.

Theoretical Basis

As implied above, the purpose of science panels is to resolve "objectively" the scientific elements of a technical dispute. The basis for the legitimacy of science panel findings lies in the assumption of scientific objectivity and neutrality.

The desired result of science panel proposals is an attempted depoliticization of science policy controversies. Thus, the theoretical basis for science panels is technocracy. Villmoare (1982, 13) writes:

> " 'Depoliticization is the ideology of technology itself' because the technocratic environment transforms political conflicts and goals into issues of technical means. The technocratic state assumes the ends of society as given, does not reexamine them, and relies primarily on scientific and administrative experts to determine effective alternatives."

By contrast, the theoretical foundation of regulatory negotiation is corporatist. Corporatism relies on group representatives to negotiate political solutions. There is no sense of objective resolution of issues, but a clear reliance on value resolution. Villmoare's description captures the essence of the corporatist category in the judicial context:

Corporatist capacity is typified by a purpose, instrumentally rational role orientation and by the ability to be politically effective . . . .In this context, the competent judge is active and imaginative in fashioning political solutions where conflict is minimized. Further, the judge is not concerned with limiting government power or drawing the line between public and private spheres of life. The corporatist judiciary encourages public and private representatives to work together to plan and execute policy effectively (Villmoare 1982, 13).

Structure

The two proposals differ considerably in their structural components. The science panel is a more permanent institution than regulatory negotiation commissions, but would differ from currently existing agency review mechanisms. Among these mechanisms are: extra-agency mechanisms (e.g., Food Safety Council, Interagency Regulatory Liaison Group); bilateral separation, where one agency sets standard while another implements them (e.g., Nuclear Regulatory Commission, EPA) agency advisory mechanisms (e.g., Scientific Advisory Panels for pesticide regulation by EPA, Chronic Hazards Advisory Panel for CPSA); and intramural separation (e.g., Office of Health and Environmental Assessment in EPA) (National Research Council 1982). Science panels would be centralized government-wide, though composition of the panels might differ depending upon the specific science panel proposal and the particular issue.

Regulatory negotiation, by contrast, is more ad hoc. That is, a negotiation panel or commission would come into existence upon the recommendation of an agency to discuss a specific issue (i.e., a proposed rule). One possible modification would employ a more permanent organizational structure within each agency or perhaps outside of any specific agency, similar to centralized science panels. This permanent structure would include a consistent set of members who would participate in regulatory negotiation on a regular basis. During the negotiations, the "rule of reason" would be employed: open discussion, sharing of information and good faith participation by all (Select Committee 1980). After the deliberations of the ad hoc version of the panel have been completed, the group disbands. In a sense, regulatory negotiation is a process rather than a structure.

Participants

Centralized science panels and regulatory negotiation differ with regard to the type of participants involved. Because the purpose of the science panel is to improve the scientific basis of agency decision-making, the panels would be composed of technical experts, eminent scientists from various disciplines. They could also employ outside consultants on advisory panels for particular issues. Panel members and consultants would not be representatives of narrow (e.g., industrial or consumer) interests but neutral experts.

In contrast, participants in regulatory negotiation would represent various affected interests and employ negotiating rather than technical skills. In addition, there are provisions for limited agency participation, for a convenor (someone to call the session and select participants) such as the chairman of the Administrative Conference, and a mediator or chairman of each negotiating panel.

In the case of both science panels and negotiations, the number of participants would be deliberately limited to facilitate the process. For example, negotiating panels with over fifteen members are likely to be unwieldly. One implication of this limitation is that selection of participants must be carefully done to provide for adequate representation of substantially affected interests. S. 1360, The Regulatory Negotiation Act, stated that in the environmental area at least one third of the participants should be businessmen and at least one third must represent worker groups. Because of the objectivity with which science panels are to operate, this interest representation is seen as unnecessary.

Outcomes

Centralized science panels would not generate scientific data; rather they would evaluate existing evidence. The result of the panel's deliberations would be a quantitative and qualitative risk assessment of potential harm posed by a technology, an analysis of the adequacy of the available data, and recommendations to the agency based on determinations of facts. H.R. 638, The National Science Council Act, required the agencies to abide by the Council's decisions on questions of fact. The Office of Science and Technology Policy (OSTP) proposal recommended that the final decisions of an agency be reviewed for consistency with the conclusions reached during the technical stages (Calkins et al. 1980).

The outcome of regulatory negotiations is more complex. The desired result is a recommendation from the negotiating panel or commission to the agency. One important consideration with regulatory negotiations is that the controversy be ripe for decisions to provide sufficient pressure on the panel to ensure the members' cooperation in the endeavor and that the panel's deliberations will be meaningful. For example, the process would be appropriate in situations where a major law has been enacted, but proposed rules have not yet been issued; where final rules have been issued but are likely to undergo substantial revision; where basic changes in legislation are likely to occur; or where court decisions have changed the interpretation of statutory mandates (47 Federal Register 30708; Harter

1982; Vig this volume). As with the science panels, agencies would have to consider the negotiating commission's recommendations (Bingham 1981).

Assumptions

Various assumptions underlie the two sets of institutional mechanisms. The assumptions are important because they, again, allow us to understand the essential differences between science panels and regulatory negotiations and also permit us to assess the likelihood of the success of particular proposals. If these assumptions are unrealistic, or unlikely to occur, then the proposals, should they be implemented, will fail.

Science Panels

Those proposing centralized science panels assert that risk management decisions have been based on poor scientific evidence. The assumption here is that science panels will produce better scientific evidence, or at least better evaluations of available evidence. The next three assumptions are related: that technical and political elements of risk decisions can be separated, that experts can resolve many technical disagreements, and that, therefore, science panels can limit the range of disagreements to policy rather than technical areas.

How realistic are these assumptions? They are realistic to the extent that definitive technical judgments can be made. But if the scientific evidence is inconclusive, because hazards posed by technologies are often chronic in nature (therefore appearing a long time following initial exposure), causal linkages are difficult to establish (Rushefsky 1982). If this be the case, it would then follow that technical experts will not be able to resolve disagreements and, equally as important, the fact/value distinction would no longer hold (Mazur 1973). If this is true, then the ability of science panels to both produce better decisions and depoliticize risk controversies is in doubt.

Criticisms of the intrusion of political values into the technical determination phase, inherent in the two-stage model of risk assessment which explicitly separates these activities (see the American Industrial Health Council quote above), really demonstrate the inevitable intermingling of facts and values. Technical determination of risk depends upon a series of asssumptions about the use of certain kinds of tests, extrapolations from tests, the kinds of models employed, etc. Different assumptions produce different technical assessments of risks and much of the controversy over proposed or actual rules concern the appropriate assumptions (Matheny and Williams 1983). Thus, proposals for a centralized science panel as a means of reducing conflict and separating factual from value considerations are inherently flawed.

Regulatory Negotiation

Regulatory negotiation similarly rests on a set of assumptions. One assumption, really a proposition based in fact, is that all parties are unhappy with the results of risk management as it presently stands. This is indicated by the frequent resort to courts by various interests challenging agency decisions. The turn to the courts to settle technical disputes concerns many people and led Judge Markey to his recommendation to employ the congressional Office of Technology Assessment as a science panel (in U.S. Congress, Joint Hearings 1980; see also Nyhart 1981).

The next two assumptions follow from the first. Technical experts will not defuse risk controversies for many of the reasons stated above. The scientific evidence is often inconclusive and consumer, environmental, public interest, and other groups oppose the science panel proposal (for fear of an industry bias) and deny the ability of the panels to separate facts and values (Office of Technology Assessment 1981). The current process, because it is adversarial in nature (for example, permitting disputants to address the agency or the courts but not each other), polarizes risk controversies. Both of these statements mean that neighter the present structure or decision-making nor science panels will produce acceptable results.

The last three assumptions point to the virtues of regulatory negotiations. By allowing representatives of groups to meet and interact face-to-face, the potential for greater understanding of the positions of the various parties is increased. This greater understanding in turn can lead to recognition of many areas of agreement. One implication of this process is the reduction of polarization and its replacement with polycentric views— there are not just two diametrically opposite views but many different perspectives, some only shades apart. Finally, to the extent that agencies act upon recommendations of negotiation panels, those decisions will be more acceptable because of the participation of interest groups (Gusman 1981; Harter 1982). Thus the outcome of regulatory negotiation is more than just a recommendation; it also includes greater understanding, consensus, and legitimacy.

Despite these advantages, regulatory negotiation will be successful only under certain conditions such as the ripeness of decisions and the good faith participation mentioned above. A group or interest with a nonnegotiable demand may cause the process to break down. The group may then withdraw from the panel and denounce any agreement the panel produces as unsatisfactory. Equity considerations may also present some difficulties. Business interests would likely bring more information and expertise to the negotiating sessions than consumer, environmental, or labor groups would be able to muster, creating an information imbalance. One can also envision problems in representation on the panels, problems that might raise the question of the legitimacy of the enterprise. Because of the limited size of the panels, some interests may not be represented. Will those interests accept decisions to which they had no part? As with many other institutions and processes, regulatory negotiation will be efficacious only if affected interests want it to be.

A related problem is one fundamental to the corporatist concept, the theoretical basis for regulatory negotiation. The notion of corporatism assumes that a particular person(s) is representative of a sector in terms of values, opinions and interests, and membership. In the case of consumer or environmental groups, no peak association exists that could claim to be representative of that sector. And even where peak associations exist, internal conflict among constituent groups limits the unity with which that association can act. In a highly pluralistic society, it becomes difficult to obtain consensus on someone as representative of a particular interest (Salisbury 1979).

A final problem with regulatory negotiation is that it may be subverted by agencies which employ this process as a means of co-opting citizen groups. Selznick (1949), in his classic study of the Tennessee Valley Authority (TVA), demonstrated how that agency was able to obtain the cooperation or at least acquiescence of the residents by bringing onto the boards a "representative" group of citizens. The representatives then became committed to TVA programs and were used to legitimize TVA actions. In a similar way, regulatory negotiation can be used to manage or control environmental groups through various restrictions as to what is negotiable and what procedures will be employed. Negotiation, then, can be a two-edged sword (Amy 1982).

CONCLUSION

At their best, science panels could create incentives for enhancing the quality of scientific evidence, improving the evaluation of available evidence and making definitive and acceptable risk assessments. At a minimum, science panels could distinguish scientific from those that are transscientific issues or incapable of technical resolution (Weinberg 1972).

The limitation of the centralized science panel proposals is that they probably will not defuse controversy. The fact that labor, consumer, and environmental interests oppose the idea is by itself sufficient grounds for skepticism of the success of the concept, undoubtedly because it represents an unrealistic attempt to separate technical risk assessment from the political aspects. The elitist, technocratic nature of science panels might make them suspect politically as a means of settling public problems, and some of these proposals could potentially be abused. The recent allegations concerning the "private science courts" or negotiations between EPA and industry interests concerning formaldehyde and DEHP raise disturbing questions about the objectivity and fairness of these procedures

(Warren and Sandler 1981; Sandler 1982; "Agency Criticized" 1982; Rushefsky, in progress). Regulatory negotiation can also be manipulated to produce and legitimize desired results.

Regulatory negotiation is a different structure from the science panel proposals. It is based on a pluralist view of conflict and social change and seeks to involve the major parties to a dispute (Crowfoot 1980). Under certain conditions, regulatory negotiation might prove valuable and reduce the adversarial nature of regulatory processes. Where the issues are specific, where decisions are pending that could be influenced by the outcome of negotiations, where parties are adequately represented and negotiate in good faith, it may be a particularly effective approach.

But negotiation too has its limits. Where those conditions do not hold, negotiation will not cure problems of the risk management process. Science panel and regulatory negotiation proposals would still leave a substantial portion of policymaking to the current system, including agencies and courts. Both proposals also fail to resolve the fact/value problem. Science panels, by employing neutral experts, violate or ignore the values context of risk management decisions. Similarly, regulatory negotiation, by deliberately involving interested parties and seeking compromise among them, diminishes the factual nature of risk management decisions. Both sets of proposals fail to come to grip with the inevitable synthesis of facts and values, and rely instead on a model of risk assessment based on an artificial separation of technical assessment and political determination.

Still, regulatory negotiation promises to increase the legitimacy of regulatory decisions and reduce societal tensions, perhaps more so than science panels. Such a result would accord with Lindblom's classic statement that the test of a good policy is agreement (Lindblom 1959).

> To the extent that Congress delegates polycentric, multiple criteria problems to regulatory agencies (and, for better or for worse, such delegations are likely to continue), some form of structured bargaining appears to comprise an essential element of any problem-solving mechanism. Such problems are at root neither technical nor legal but political—that is to say, they are problems of social choice in a world of ever more limited resources. In such a world, bargaining may do for us what litigation and law increasingly cannot: it may nourish those impulses toward accommodation, reconciliation, and mutuality of interests which an adversary society tends to stifle, but without which no society can effectively discharge its business. (Schuck 1979, 34).

NOTES

1. The author would like to thank the following people for providing information and assistance in researching this article: Gail Bingham, Sam Gusman, David Pritzker, Philip Harter, Lester Brown and Larry McGray. The author would also like to thank his colleagues Albert Matheny and Walter Rosenbaum for their assistance and comments on earlier drafts of this chapter.

2. Timothy B. Clark "Costs V. Benefits." *National Journal* 13 (August 1, 1981): 1382-1386.

3. *The New York Times,* May 29, 1983.

4. These distinctions are based on discussions with Gail Bingham of the Conservation Foundation. The Foundation publishes a quarterly newsletter, *Resolve,* that provides information about negotiation events and groups around the country. For a discussion of site specific disputes, see Lake 1980. For examples of intervention, see Select Committee on Small Business 1890 and Gusman 1981

5. Remarks by the Vice President of the United States before the Twenty-Third Plenary Session, Administrative Conference of the United States. Washington, D.C., December 10, 1981.

6. *The New York Times,* May 29, 1983.

Chapter 9

DISAGREEING ABOUT RISK:
THE INSTITUTIONAL CULTURES OF RISK MANAGEMENT
AND PLANNING FOR FUTURE GENERATIONS[1]
Steve Rayner

Editor's Introduction

The last paper in the book provides a perspective different from any of the others; perhaps this is because the author is an anthropologist. Rather than suggesting any new institutional arrangements for controlling risk, Rayner devotes his attention to four subcultures within our society. Each subculture prefers a different basis for assessing and controlling technological risks, and each therefore is associated with different kinds of institutions.

If we accept Rayner's thesis that these different cultural perspectives all participate to some extent in selecting public risk control strategies, then we can see that a two-stage model is not adequate to comprehend the complex political and economic sparring that must surround each policy decision. In fact, implicitly Rayner endorses a procedure something like regulatory negotiation, because it provides representation not only for diverse interests but for affected groups that ordinarily might not participate actively in such choices. He also explicitly criticizes the two-stage model because it serves the needs of only one or two of the subcultures.

Rayner touches on many of the themes discussed by the other authors. Rather than reaching any conclusions about them, however, his paper serves to stimulate the reader to ask additional questions. In that way, it opens the way for new research on the relationships between risk policy, scientific information, and institutions. It thus provides a fitting conclusion to a book that has that same purpose.

150

WHEN RISKS MUST BE MANAGED BY INSTITUTIONS

There are deep divisions among the public and within the scientific community over the acceptability of a wide variety of potentially hazardous technologies. In facing these controversies, the foremost challenge to risk managers in the scientific establishment, in industry, and in government is to determine what levels of perceived risk are publicly acceptable in situations where individuals are unable to negotiate a satisfactory solution for themselves. Such situations arise in at least four kinds of circumstances.

The first is due to *isolation*. In this case, individuals could reduce risk by their own actions if others would act similarly to forego a benefit. But, in the absence of some sort of mechanism to ensure the cooperation of others, individual decisions to modify behavior will be ineffective. An example of such a case would be improving road safety by driving slower. Experience tells us that in the absence of institutionally enforced speed limits this is unlikely to occur.

The second case is that in which *transaction costs* of individual solutions may prove to be too high for individuals to negotiate their own solutions. This may occur either because many people are creating small risks that are unacceptable in the aggregate, or because a few people impose a large risk that is widely distributed over many others. An example of the former of these problems is that of air pollution from private cars, while the latter is illustrated by air pollution from industrial plants.

Perhaps the most common case facing risk managers is when *irreconcilable interests* in large-scale projects to provide public goods make it difficult or impossible to achieve a social concensus about safety. This often seems to be the case when planning the construction of nuclear power plants.

The final case is that of *preemption,* where decisions have already been made by previous generations, or where future generations will be affected by the decisions made today. This case is well exemplified in public controversies over nuclear or toxic chemical waste (EPA 1979; Ausness 1979).

In all of these cases, decisions must be made by institutions, often those of governments but also of trade unions, professional and scientific associations, and the judiciary. The particular problems of each case are ubiquitious in the formulation of public policy where they are often highlighted because they involve life and death decisions which arouse considerable public and media concern. But in the fourth case, that of planning for future generations, there are particularly taxing problems facing institutional decision-makers, whether they are moral philosophers, industrialists, technologists, politicians, or the people from the town meeting.

Preemption is one of the least well understood of the four problems of institutional risk management that I have listed. This is because it raises particular difficulties in obtaining consent from those who are not yet born, and distributing liabilities among those who made the original decision, but have since passed away. It is certainly an issue that is beset by the most emphatically expressed moral arguments. For this reason, I have chosen to emphasize this case to illustrate the different approaches to institutional decision-making that come into conflict in the course of risk policy debates. I intend to untangle these moral arguments in the course of this paper, and to show the cultural basis of each viewpoint.

SOME FALLACIES IN TECHNOLOGICAL DECISION-MAKING

The problems of all four cases that require institutional decision-making are compounded in dealing with new technologies by the fact that the risks may be poorly understood, even by scientific experts (Douglas and Wildavsky 1982; Rushefsky 1982). This raises further problems about determining and relying upon a consensus of either public or expert perceptions. How then can institutions manage risks in a way that is socially acceptable?

To date, science and technology policymaking has been dominated by a three-stage process of risk management. This starts with inventories of activities, then attempts to establish discrepancies between public perceptions and expert assessments of the probabilities and extent of hazards, and finally aims to educate the public either to avoid the danger or to accept that the mechanisms that the experts have devised are adequate to reduce risk to an acceptable level. [2]

The problem with this approach to risk management, of closing the perception gap between public perceptions and the real risk as it is assessed by the experts, is that it is based on the highly questionable assumption that expert perceptions represent reality unmediated by sociocultural conditions—as if experts suspend the essentially social basis of being human while making professional judgments. This assumption was a highly visible feature of the presentaton of both legal and technical submissions to the public inquiry into the proposed construction of the nuclear reprocessing plant at Windscale in the UK (Wynne 1982).

Whitehead (1926) would have recognized the experts' faith in their knowledge of the world as a case of what he called the fallacy of misplaced concreteness; the belief that we can gain access to raw unmediated reality. As De Finetti (1974) points out, a probability estimate is always somebody's probability. One's degree of belief in an outcome is based only on information selected as relevant from that which is available, while there is no way of ever knowing if even all the available knowledge is sufficient, let alone complete (Clark 1980). The probability estimates of risk analysts are based on observations of repeatable events, yet few, if any, events are truly repeatable. The throw of a die may come close, but the same horserace can never be run twice.

If the numerical determination of probability in risk assessment is subjective, how much more so is the evaluation of any given probability as high or low. The recognition of a particular combination of probability and magnitude as a risk is relatively independent of what an expert might determine that probability and magnitude to be. For example, the determination of the outcomes as utilities or costs is highly subjective. Lovins (1977, 914) demonstrates the ambiguous character of attributes in an entertaining discussion of how different values lead to different characterizations of the same thing. "Is an artful new kind of synthetic dessert a benefit or a disgrace?"

Psychologists tell us that dread, familiarity and exposure seem to be just as important to risk evaluations as probability or magnitude (Slovic, Fischhoff and Lichtenstein 1980). Although death may be lurking around each corner, the risk of death does not exist apart from someone's perception of it.

Unfortunately, even the psychologists who study individual risk perceptions often slip into the same error as those mathematicians and engineers who equate probability with risk. In their descriptions of risk-averse and accepting individuals of probability overestimators and underestimators and tendencies to prefer large losses that are only probable to small certain losses (Kahneman, Slovic, and Tversky 1982), they retain as their yardstick the experts' assessments of the real risks.

Just as the experts' error has been to ignore the subjectivity of their own risk perceptions, the psychologists may have erred in placing the main burden of that subjectivity on the shoulders of misperceiving individuals. Our subjectivity in perceiving risk may have less to do with our innate psychological disabilities than with our learned social dispositions. We live in a world of social processes, and risks, including what estimates of probability or magnitude really mean to different people, are qualities conferred on expectations of the future by social processes.

To understand the social processes by which risk qualities are conferred on events, we must turn to the sociology of perception which tells us that a person's recognition of what constitutes a risk, as well as his estimates of what level of that risk is acceptable, is influenced by his ideals. In turn, his ideals are cultural constructs that are deeply rooted in the individual's place in society's institutions.

When sections of the public believe that science and technology have the potential to cause widespread or catastrophic loss, policymakers are faced with problems that lie at the heart of distributive justice. In making preemptive decisions on behalf of future generations who can neither be consulted about the principles of distribution, nor call us to account for our actions, these problems are far more acute. Whether today's scientists or public judge a given set of liabilities to be acceptable partly depends on their perceptions of what the good society should be like. The institutions of the good society as it is regarded by future generations may be very different from those cherished by today's decision-makers. Indeed, even within the present generation we see that the different social and moral principles upheld by institutions affect their members' judgments of what dangers are to be most feared, what risks are worth taking, and who should be allowed to take them.

It would be surprising, therefore, if there were no discrepancies in the assessments of different experts and between these and the fears of the lay public. Furthermore, the discrepancies may prove to be better accounted for by the culture of experts' institutions and the cultures of lay publics than by the dichotomy between informed experts' perceptions and those of uniformed lay persons. By starting with expert risk assessments, the current wisdom of risk management may be putting the cart before the horse, because deep disagreement on principles of social justice can be the source of discrepancies in the calculation of probabilities and values.

THREE INSTITUTIONAL CULTURES OF RISK MANAGEMENT

Cultural analyses of risk perception, such as those of Douglas and Wildavsky (1982), Gross and Rayner (1983), and Michael Thompson (1981; 1982) indicate that the social organization of the institutions and communities concerned, rather than the risks themselves, determine the policy process. People experiencing different forms of social organization maintain different principles for recognizing a risk, for obtaining social consent to it, and for the distribution of liabilities and benefits arising from it. This view of the relationship between technology and society has even reached the ears of the U.S. Congress. "Maybe we need a kind of assessment that looks at a human value system and how it impacts technology rather than starts with technology." (OTA 1976, 203) Surely risk management should, therefore, start with a choice of organizing principles and not with a choice between disasters.

There seem to be three main kinds of decision-makers whose interests incline each one to favor a coherent, but apparently incompatible, set of principles for achieving consent to technological risk and for determining the distribution of losses and gains (Calabresi, 1977; Cyert and March 1963; Olsen 1965). This package of principles and perceptions is what I mean by an *institutional culture* of risk management. In what follows, I will show how a principle of liability in each case is implied by a corresponding principle of political consent arising from three kinds of institution or social organization, each one sustaining one of the matching models in legal and political philosophy. The organization of each type of social system makes its members sensitive to different fears.

Since these are all Weberian ideal types (Weber 1947), they are models of the logical possibilities of institutional structure. Weber does not claim that any principle of behavior demonstrated by an ideal type will have an exact empirical counterpart. Each type is intended to evoke the extreme features in a typology, so that empirical cases may be laid out in between.

The first type of institutional or social system is variously described as entrepreneurial, competitive, or market organization. Here, everyone is expected to work hard at developing his own specialty which he can market to others. Organization is ego centered. The individual carefully maintains his own networks with those who need his particular and rare talents. He will also cultivate contacts with specialists in other fields on whom he can call for help with tasks that are outside of his own specialty. The experts in high technology who act as consultants to bureaucratic or political policymakers might favor this kind of social organization, as will entrepreneurial businessmen or jet-set academics. In American nuclear politics, the entrepreneurial viewpoint is strongly represented among the equipment manufacturers such as General Electric and Westinghouse (Pringle and Spigelman 1981, ch 16).

As in all market systems, uncertainty is an intrinsic element in the social transactions of entrepreneurs. To maintain credibility in the ideas market, the competitive individual relies on continued success. He must always innovate, or push back the boundaries of his special skill or knowledge a little further. Decisions about risks in these sorts of institutions will, therefore, tend to be expert adaptive judgments constrained by the minimum of formal procedures. Competitive pressures restrict the use of time in this context, so the perceived consequences of delay or procrastination are likely to encourage calculated risk taking.

The second type of organization is bureaucratic (Weber 1947), or hierarchical. It is organic in the sense that it consists of differentiated roles, each of which is seen to contribute to the functioning of the whole. These kinds of institutions are bound by rules and there is likely to be an emphasis on the procedures of decision making. Conflicting goals and interests are combined, without being resolved, in routine procedures (Cyert and March 1963). Career success consists of rising through a hierarchy of qualifications and grades. In seeking promotions, the candidate needs to convince his superiors that he has successfully internalized the necessary skills, and rules for their application. Organizations such as the pronuclear Scientists and Engineers for Secure Energy, laboratory and plant administrations, and established regulatory agencies such as the U.S. Social Security Agency, are good examples of this type.

A characteristic of this sort of organization is that risks are likely to be routinized as far as possible. Properly constituted bodies decide what dangers are, and what procedures are appropriate to minimize them. When accidents do occur, mechanisms for finding facts, compensating victims, and reviewing procedures are on hand. The routine apportionment of time resources to specific tasks may tend to encourage a diminished sense of their urgency. Thus, a small hazard may increase because bureaucracies respond slowly to danger (Lawless 1974; Rosenbaum, this volume).

The third type of institution is the egalitarian group. Olsen (1965) points out that communities that adopt this kind of organization tend to be small for organizational reasons. Solidarity is *mechanical* in that it is based on everyone being the same and identifying with like others. Unlike market organization, the emphasis here is on cooperation rather than on competition. The group's smallness is inimical to the development of bureaucracy. Decisions are made by consensus wherever possible. Everyone is held responsible for the welfare of everyone else in the group, and solidarity is the highest value (Rayner 1982).

Some political and religious sects, as well as groups like the Clamshell Alliance that maintain total opposition to capital intensive technologies because they require the concentration of power in large corporations or central government, are known to favor this kind of organization (Douglas and Wildavsky 1982).

The potential hazards of high technology are a more promising rallying cry for these groups among the wider society than direct attacks on accepted institutions and the concept of sustained economic growth. Participants in public policy debates, who draw on a background in egalitarian groups, are likely to be more sensitive to risk and be on the lookout for technological hazards where representatives of market or bureaucratic institutions might incorporate or discount them respectively. Hence, they may fulfill an early warning role for the rest of society.

Each of these three institutional types is summarized in Table 9. The social organization of each type of system makes its members sensitive to different sorts of fears and will in turn lead them to favor one of three distinctive attitudes to risk bearing and, as a consequence, three different risk management strategies also shown in Table 9. In particular, the preferred spread of liabilities and benefits and the favored means of obtaining consent will vary between the three kinds of organizations. These two components of each risk management strategy are of special importance for the problem of planning for future generations.

Policymakers in market organizations will be likely to favor a *revealed preference* (Thaler and Rosen 1975) approach for obtaining consent—sometimes called *implicit consent* (MacLean 1980)—which allows the consumer to buy as much safety as he is prepared to pay for. Smoke detectors are available through the market to all those who are prepared to pay for the higher level of fire protection that they afford. When pure market solutions are not available, institutions of this sort will attempt to reproduce what the market would have done if it had not been impeded by high information or transaction costs. Hence, in New York City, owners of apartment buildings have recently been required by law to install smoke detectors in tenants' apartments and are empowered to charge the tenant a one-time fee for doing so. This system will also favor a loss-spreading

Table 9

Three Types of Institutional Structures

Institutional Structure	Competitive/ Market	Bureaucratic/ Hierarchical	Egalitarian Group
Characteristics			
Transactional arena	Ego-based networks	Organic groups	Mechanical groups
Ideal transactional mode	Competition	Routine Procedures	Cooperation
Decision-making	Individual	Committee	Concensus
Keys to success	Innovation and timing	Promotion through grades	Internal harmony
Driving values	Expansion	System maintenance	Equality
Examples	Entrepreneurs Jet-set academics Leading politicians Big men	Large corporations Government offices Political parties East African age grade/lineage systems	Anti-nuclear protest groups (Clamshell) Alliance, etc.) Some religious and political sects
Attitudes To Risk Bearing			
Decisions about risk	Expert adaptive judgment	Routinized procedure	Extended public argument
Perceptions of risk taking	Incorporate calculated risk as legitimate costs	Diminished sensitivity and responsiveness to danger	High sensitivity and aversion to risk
Major focus of concern	Market failure	System failure	Dominance by large institutions
Preferred spread of liability/costs	Market loss spreading	Redistributive taxation	Moral determination (guilty pay)
Favored means of obtaining consent	Revealed preference—reproduce market behaviour unimpeded by transaction costs	Hypothetical consent to legitimacy of institutions allows them to decide	Expressed preference—direct consultation based on ranked values

approach to liability, in which market mechanisms determine who bears losses (Calabresi 1977).

Under these conditions, technological hazards are likely to be perceived as the legitimate and inevitable cost of the pursuit of the economic and humanitarian benefits of scientific progress. People in competitive institutions will be prepared to take high probability risks if they are likely to collect individual rewards, and will minimize the danger in arguments with hierarchical bureaucrats. The risks that they will select for attention and emphasis will be those of market failure rather than technological hazard.

Members of bureaucratic organizations favor what is sometimes called *hypothetical consent* (a Rawlsian approach). Here, the citizen is assumed to have entered into a social contract with the institution, whereby he may be deemed to assent to decisions made through the rational procedures of that institution, even though he might not like the particular outcome. The acceptability of risks will, therefore, be determined by appeals to the constitutionalilty of the institutional structures for decision making.

Policymaking in this kind of system will favor redistributive taxation as a means of apportioning liability for risk. Bureaucracies make use of redistributive mechanisms to apportion costs in a way that appears to them to be least disruptive; not to the whole of society perhaps, but certainly to those clienteles whose stability they see as important to the longevity of the institutional framework.

The routinization of risks and the diffusion of liability will tend to diminish the perception of uncertainty and the urgency of hazards as they arise. Whereas the individual competitor in the market will incorporate technological risks into his calculations, the bureaucratic pooicymaker may underestimate hazards, or even fail to perceive them at all. His main concern with risk will be that of institutional failure or the breakdown of established procedures (Rosenbaum this volume).

Egalitarian groups will favor *expressed preferences* that appeal to explicit judgments of ranked values (shared by the group) rather than to the revealed preferences or hypothetical consent approaches for determining the acceptability of risky policies that are favored respectively by entrepreneurs or hierarchists. Furthermore, members of egalitarian groups will seek a moral determination of liability that appeals to those same ranked values, rather than the market or distributive approaches to loss favored by entrepreneurs or bureaucrats. The acceptability of risky policies will therefore be determined according to criteria that are very different from those invoked by entrepreneurs or by bureaucrats.

It is important to recognize that the three kinds of decision-makers whose interests include them to prefer one principle of distribution of losses will not necessarily prefer the same principle for the distribution of gains. We have said that market society favors a loss-spreading approach to liability in which market mechanisms enable institutions to distribute their losses as widely as possible. For example, to cover the costs of the emergency shutdown of the Indian Point reactor in 1981, Consolidated Edision imposed a surcharge on its customers to avoid penalizing its shareholders. Although there is always some room in such cases for dispute about whether such an event is the fault of the operator, the builder, or the designer, no one has suggested that the customers could be held to blame for the breakdown. Nevertheless, it was they who had to foot the bill. (Elsewhere in this volume, Rosenbaum and Wood both make this point more generally about the effects of the Price-Anderson Act.) However, the entrepreneurs who make up market society will (asymmetrically) prefer the principle that allows the individual risk initiator to collect any gains that may accrue.

In hierarchical organizations, the bureaucrats will prefer to transfer losses through the system; they will (symmetrically) prefer a system of allocating benefits where they best reinforce the accepted structures (in the first case sometimes the deepest pockets and in the second, sometimes the emptiest pockets). They will not prefer the widest spread in either case of losses or gains.

Finally, the egalitarian organizations, given their strong preference for explicit moral justifications of actions and their unwillingness to allow economic or other societal interests to override those, will want to allocate costs to guilty parties but (asymmetrically) given their communal principles, they will want the broadest spread of gains (see Table 10). Indeed, many groups with this structure are explicitly socialist or even Marxist in character.

Table 10

The Asymmetry of the Desired Distributiion of Losses and Gains

Institutional Structure	Competitive/ Market	Bureaucratic/ Hierarchical	Egalitarian Group
Desired spread of loss	Broadest—market loss spreading	Institutional loss party	Narrowest—faulty
Desired spread of gains	Narrowest— rewards for enterprise	Institutional provision of goods	Broadest—redistribution of wealth and resources

From the contrast between the three institutional cultures engaged in technology policy debates, it is clear that risk-managing institutions within each type of institutional culture will have great difficulty in understanding the fears and objections of the others. In particular, given the asymmetry of the desired spread of risks and benefits, and the fundamentally incompatible approaches to the question of consent, each is unlikely to be able to offer a package of compensations for risk bearing that would satisfy a clientele with experience of one of the other types of social organization and corresponding culture. The problems are exacerbated, as we shall shortly see, when the risks are known to fall on future generations which cannot give consent to a decision that may preempt their own preference for the distribution of risks and benefits. Yet the provision of special compensation, for example to communities located close to nuclear or toxic waste dumps, is now recognized by risk managers as an increasingly important requirement in the design of control systems for modern technological hazards (Kevin 1980).

The problem is that fundamental disagreements about the principles at stake inhibit risk analysis and decision-making. The real choice for risk managers is not between expert and lay perceptions, but between alternative cultural perspectives. Once this viewpoint is accepted, it follows that we require a model of risk management that would incorporate moral and political perspectives based on a sociological understanding of the risky prospects that are most likely to capture the attention of each kind of organization. Once the organizing principles have been identified in this way, the technical assessments of probabilities and values should recede in importance in the conduct of policy debates. Preferred methods of controlling and compensating for different kinds of losses can be agreed, upon based on the deeply rooted cultural values that accompany membership of each sort of institution.

GRID/GROUP ANALYSIS

It is one thing to outline the basis of a sociological model of risk management in principle as I have done here. The task of realizing such a model in practice is much more difficult, especially in view of the fact that real societies seldom consist of the pure ideal types of institutional organization that are described here. Real societies and institutions are a mixture of these. The balance of this mixture, and who has institutionally acknowledged standing in the debates, both depend on the arena within which the debate is staged. In the United States, egalitarianism has been able, particularly during the Carter Administration, to penetrate even the Federal Government and the regulatory establishment, but it has not yet shown itself among the mandarins of Whitehall. Therefore, any sociological model of risk management must be capable of disaggregating the three types of decision-makers within complex institutions and assessing the relative strength of each type.

Fortunately there is a method of cultural analysis available to us that is capable of performing this task. It is called grid/group analysis (Gross and Rayner 1983).

Grid/group analysis starts by considering the minimum requirements of social life as postulated by political theory. It constructs a dimension for group membership out of commitment to a social unit larger than the individual, and an orthogonal grid coordinate out of the strength of social hierarchy within the social unit. Group commitment may vary between low strength where individualism is rife, to high strength where group solidarity is highly valued and enforced by sanctions. Grid is low strength where there are few hierarchical classifications constraining the behavior of individuals whether or not they are members of a close-knit social unit. High grid strength is found wherever individuals are subject to many rules and regulations concerning their behavior that are enforced either by other individuals able to impose sanctions (at low group). The two dimensions therefore generate four prototype visions of social life illustrated in Figure 3.

Three of these grid/group prototypes, labelled A, C, and D, are immediately recognizable as the ideal types of risk management institutions described in this paper. The absence of restrictions from rules or from the prior claims of others is the model for the free-market economy to be found at the extreme bottom left of the diagram. As social institutions make increasing demands of incorporation and regulation, society moves from A to C. The market may not be absent, but the further into C we go, the greater will be the control of regulators until, at the extreme top right corner, economic and all other aspects of social life are strictly controlled by centralized authority. That authority may be a church, a state, or, on a smaller scale, a patriarchal family head. Crying out against the perceived excesses of either system are the egalitarians, at D, whose aversion to risk is a plausible rallying cry for members of mainstream society who feel discomforted by the apparently blase attitudes of individualist risk takers, or of bureaucrats who may be slow to react to hazards.

Grid/group analysis also reminds us of a fourth social context that we have so far ignored. That is one in which there is no basis at all for obtaining collective consent to risks. These are the residual categories of people who are excluded from the public policy debate for one reason or another. In market organization there are people who, having no goods or services to exchange, get driven out of the market. In hierarchy, these are people not represented by the established institutions of representation. Very often they are those people who have the fewest or the least socially valued skills. Hospital porters and maintenance staff are, for example, on the lowest rungs of the medical hierarchy. Supermarket cashiers and others doing donkey work (Mars 1982) also fit this part of the grid/group model. Not all of these join small egalitarian groups. They tend to be the most vulnerable in any system.

GRID

high	**B RESIDUAL** Constrained by rules Obligations and demands imposed by classification but few resources from others Fragmented networks Risks imposed by others without consultation—passive resentment Future seen as endless repetition of operational cycles	**C BUREAUCRATIC/ HIERARCHICAL** Constrained by rules but also protected by them Many demands and resources derived from others Highly structured networks with distinct boundaries Risks routinized through established procedures—complacency Expectations of future based on past epochs marked by ancestors or great events
low	**A COMPETITIVE/MARKET** Unconstrained by rules Few demands or resources from others Ego-centered networks without boundaries Risks incorporated into portfolios of concerns—acceptance of calculated risks Future incorporated in concern for operational deadlines	**D EGALITARIAN GROUP** Unconstrained by rules Many demands and resources from others Transitive networks with distinct boundaries Risks resisted—high sensitivity to possible hazards Future epochs compressed into the present on model of short historical depth

0	low	high	GROUP

Figure 3

**Grid and Group Dimensions and Associated Attitudes
to Risk and the Future**

These residual categories are the largest category of risk bearers left uncompensated by market or hierarchy. Their interests are likely to be overriden when either system considers risk distribution. On the other hand, some egalitarian groups reinforce their perception of morality by espousing the cause of the most vulnerable sectors of the human population. Thus, these four grid/group prototypes provide the structure of risk debates in complex society (Figure 3).

Although Figure 4 indicates that we anticipate general tendencies for risk acceptance or aversion to correlate with particular types of institutional culture, opposition to specific proposals can occur in every type of institution. When it does, we expect to find what O'Hare (1977) calls not-in-my-backyard (or nimby) groups forming in high-grid cultures. An example would be the Environmental Coalition on Nuclear Power. We would expect universalist opposition groups, like the Clamshell Alliance (Douglas and Wildavsky 1982) to spring up at low grid. Entrepreneurs and residuals will generally not organize collectively of their own accord. However, we anticipate that the former will happily take advantage of any opportunity to advance their interests. While residuals will tend to be fatalistic about the outcomes of decisions over which they have no real control, they may tag along with either type of opposition movement as a way of protesting against their general powerlessness.

Ever since the introduction of the grid/group device in 1970, the taxing problem has been to devise replicable measuring techniques for each of the coordinates. Fortunately, we believe that we have to come to grips with this problem with the techniques described in Gross and Rayner (1983). We are now able to score any social unit for grid or group as the average of a number of indices that are measured on a scale between 0 and 1.

This ability to make replicable measurements gives us the potential to test the correlation of the four prototype configuratons of grid/group organizations with the institutional types that we have been discussing.

The grid/group prototypes elucidate the structure of risk debates in complex society. Our ability to measure each dimension converts the multiple insights of political philosophy, legal theory, and organizational studies into a practical tool for comparing the relative strength of different institutional cultures within complex communities.

THE PROBLEM OF PLANNING FOR FUTURE GENERATIONS

To illustrate the claim that it is a potentially valuable tool for applied policy research, I shall conclude by showing how the grid/group approach may be particularly helpful in unravelling the thorny problems of planning for future generations. Any sort of planning for the future raises different problems particular to each kind of institution, because the social organization of each leads to a strong tendency to view the future in a particular way (Rayner 1982).

In *market institutions,* expectations of the future are likely to be strongly focussed on deadlines. Success in entrepreneurial activities depends largely on timing; planning for shifting market tastes, clinching deals at the right price, meeting delivery or publishing deadlines, or knowing when to sell your pork-belly futures. The emphasis is on short-term expectations and immediate returns on activities and investments. Long-term planning is a feature of corporate institutions (whether they are African Lineages or ITT) which are, in principle, immortal. Entrepreneurs don't have time for such long-term considerations (Figure 3).

For people in *Residual Categories,* the future appears as an endless repetition of daily routines. Lacking the resources for future investment or to underwrite their escape from their lot, members of residual categories have little to look forward to that would focus their attention on long-term futures. The rarity of events that engage collectivities, such as rites of passage, festivals, celebrations of historical events, characteristic of high-grid/high-group institutions, provides an impoverished model for differentiating the future.

In *bureaucratic/hierarchical* institutions, history is strongly differenti-ated, in marked contrast with both previous types of social organizations. Anniversaries of great events in the past are celebrated collectively and provide models for discriminating epochs of the future. Clear recognition of age-sets and generations, which are the basis of establishing seniority in the present, also engender clear expectations of an ordered future. The regimes of distinguished leaders (whether kings or company directors) also contri-bute to an expectation of the future.

In *egalitarian groups* too, history tends to be viewed as epochal but, because of the problems of resolving disputes in social organizations which are aggressively egalitarian (and therefore dismissive of dispute resolution by claims to seniority or appeals to established procedures) those groups tend to frequent schism. Consequently, they have a foreshortened historical memory typical, for example, of the leftist utopian groups in the UK (Rayner 1982). The ideas of the founding ancestors are considered to be literally true for the present. Both Marx and the Bible are subject to the most profoundly fundamentalist interpretations. The group's crusading mission may lead to a sense of historical self-importance that results in the view that the present epoch is the decisive historical moment. Hence, the prevalence of militarian expectations amongst organizations of this sort, and anti-nuclear groups' susceptibility to prophesies of doom.

These expectations of the future give rise to quite different attitudes to risks that are known to affect future generations. These attitudes are particu-larly focussed on the problem of obtaining consent and on the asymmetry of desired distribution of losses and gains, as summarized in Figure 4.

GRID

	B RESIDUAL	C BUREAUCRATIC/ HIERARCHICAL
high	*Consent* — risks are imposed on present generation without consent so why should the future be different *Liability* —similar fatalism about bearing costs of other people's errors	*Consent* — assumed that future generations will recognize same institutions *Liability* — all long-term planning is for future system maintenance. System must be strong enough to cushion unforseen future costs
low	A COMPETITIVE/MARKET *Consent* — assumed that future generations will make decisions on current market condition and will therefore accept similar decisions of predecessors *Liability* — emergence of future liabilities can be left to market forces when they occur. Provide stimulus for future enterprise	D EGALITARIAN GROUP *Consent* — direct consultation with future generations is impossible therefore we violate their rights (and our principles) by imposing risks on them *Liability* — benefits (if recognized seen as short-term and accruing to individuals or institutions. Costs will fall on future generations who will be unable to make the guilty pay

0   low   high   GROUP

Figure 4

Planning for Future Generations in Each Type of Institutional Culture

A. In *Market organizations* inter-temporal responsibility receives little recognition. If future generations are not adaptive or innovative enough to deal with the legacy of today's technology, then they probably don't deserve to survive.
B. In *Residual categories* inter-temporal responsibility is someone else's affair, "I've enough to do trying to get by myself."
C. In *Bureaucratic institutions* inter-temporal responsibility is strong but institutionally safeguarded provided those institutions are themselves nurtured and kept healthy.
D. In *Egalitarian groups,* inter-temporal responsibility is strong, but people have no trust in institutions. You might hear them say, "If we cannot obtain consent from future generations and if our descendants cannot force long dead decision-makers to pay for their errors, then we have no right to accept risks on behalf of those descendants."

Hitherto, proposals to provide incentives to risk bearers to host a hazardous technology, such as a high-level nuclear waste facility, have concentrated on providing monetary payments (LaPorte 1978) and have stressed the relationships between the Federal Government and the States concerned, rather than the host communities (Kevin 1980; Lee 1980). This is probably because legal precedents for compensation have been based on redressing damage actually suffered. There is some difficulty in establishing which communities around a site, and which members of those communities should receive payment in the absence of demonstrable loss (O'Hare 1977).

It has recently been proposed, however, that it may be more appropriate to design incentive packages containing more than just monetary payments (O'Connor 1980; Carnes et al. 1984). Furthermore, the same authors recognize that such a package should be responsive to the diverse, and possibly competing, concerns within and between the communities actually affected. The addition of a grid/group perspective to these proposals would enable us to go further than just arguing that the organizational cultures of the communities must be taken into account when risk-managing institutions design packages of compensating benefits for long-term risk bearing. We can actually suggest a cultural basis for the design of such packages. For example:

A. *Market cultures* will require a greater emphasis on *short-term* rewards. They will look for actions designed to bring extra benefits to communities that assume risks on behalf of the wider society. These might include direct monetary payments tax incentives, and the location of desirable projects as well as risky ones in the vicinity.
B. *Residuals* will probably have to put up with whatever they are offered. However, we should question the morality of taking advantage of their vulnerability. If we do not, they may turn to the the Egalitarian Groups in protest. Then the risk managers' problems multiply.

C. *Hierarchists* will require a greater emphasis on system maintenance and investments in the community that will ensure that future controls over hazardous activities are adequate and that compensation for unforeseen contingencies will be forthcoming. A suitable package might include support for the community infrastructure in the form of investment in public works, such as new schools. Land value guarantees might be welcome as promoting community stability, while guaranteed trust funds and insurance schemes could compensate those who actually suffer in the event of an accident or anomaly arising.

D. *Egalitarians* will not willingly accept any risk to future generations because (1) they are prone to catastrophic views of the future and (2) because such risks violate their most cherished ethical principles with respect to both compensation and the distribution of liabilities.

   However, actions to mitigate the risks might help to reassure those whose commitment to low-grid/high-group principles is less than total. Measures designed to prevent, reduce, or eliminate adverse consequences before they occur might include the provision of buffer zones, community controlled monitoring, and the right of the community to shut down the operation if negotiated safety thresholds are breached.

With the introduction of measurable grid/group scales, designing packages of compensations to account for the differing perceptions of how to manage risks that impose costs on future generations becomes *plausible*. Whether or not it is *practicable* will depend on the ability of institutions charged with risk management to suspend their own way of looking at the problem to accommodate the views of those for which they are planning.

This approach to long-term planning has been questioned for having overtones of social engineering or of bribing some people to carry the can for the rest of us. My own view is that applied cultural analysis of risk debates has the potential to extend informed public participation in the decision making process. Grid/group analysis shows how people from different institutional backgrounds may otherwise talk past each other because they maintain different culturally conditioned perceptual filters that admit concerns relevant to their day-to-day experience while blocking those ideas that are irrelevant or would place obstacles in the way of their daily lives. By making the basis of this disagreement explicit, we might alert policymakers to weak or distant voices which might not otherwise be noticed.

In the final analysis, our sympathy for the cultural approach to risk analysis, as well as our view of the morality of providing incentive packages to risk bearers will likely depend on our own experiences of an institutional culture of the sort described by the grid/group model. What I have tried to do here is to clarify the issues and the essentially cultural basis of the arguments that are brought to bear on them. This is not a solution to the dilemmas of risk management in general or to the problem of planning for future generations in particular. It is a starting point for discussion.

NOTES

1.   I should like to thank the friends and colleagues who took part in seminars on this theme in the Department of Sociology and Social Anthropology at Keele University, the Cornell University Science Technology and Society Program, and the Energy Division of the Oak Ridge National Laboratory.

My special gratitude goes to Douglas MacLean of the University of Maryland, Davydd Greenwood of Cornell, and Susan Hadden of the University of Texas at Austin for their detailed critiques of earlier versions of this paper.

Thanks also to Heather Hill of Boston University School of Public Health, who was kind enough to retype the manuscript more than once while I was a visiting scholar there.

2.   Editor's note. Rayner's ''Three-Stage'' process differs only slightly from the two-stage process criticized by others. It is also dominated by the scientific part of risk analysis; indeed, Rayner distinguishes three different ways in which this occurs.

REFERENCES

[Ed. Note: In addition to serving as the list of works cited in the text, this bibliography is intended to provide the reader with a general introduction to the literature on risk, especially risk and institutions. Works of more limited relevance, especially government reports on special topics, are described in the footnotes of the chapters in which they are cited.]

Aberbach, Joel D. Changes in Congressional Oversight. In Carol H. Weiss and Allen H. Barton (Eds.), *Making Bureaucracies Work*, Beverly Hills, California: Sage Publications, 1980.

Ackerman, Bruce A. and William T. Hassler, *Clean Coal/Dirty Air*. New Haven: Yale University Press 1981.

Alliance of American Insurers, et al. Nuclear Power, Safety and Insurance: Issues of the 1980s: The Insurance Industry's Viewpoint. Available from American Nuclear Insurers, Farmington, Conn.

American Industrial Health Council. *Comments On a Report of the Interagency Regulatory Liaison Group* (IRLG), Work Group on Risk Assessment Entitled "Scientific Bases for Identification of Potential Carcinogens and Estimation of Risks." Scarsdale, N.Y.: American Industrial Health Council, Inc. 1979.

American Industrial Health Council. *AIHC Proposal for a Science Panel*. Scarsdale, N.Y.: American Industrial Health Council, Inc. 1980.

Amy, Douglas J. Environmental Mediation: A New Approach with some Old Problems. *Citizen Participation*, November-December 1982, *4(2)*, 10−11, 24.

Andrews, Richard N.L. Cost-Benefit Analysis, Deregulation and Environmental Policy. In Norman J. Vig and Michael E. Kraft (Eds.), *Environmental Policy in the 1980s: The Impact of the Reagan Administration*, Washington, D.C.: Congressional Quarterly Press, forthcoming, 1984.

Anthony, Robert. Accountability and Credibility in the Management of Complex Hazardous Technology. *Policy Studies Review*, May 1982, *1(4)*, 705−715.

Arnould, Richard J. and Henry Grabowski. Automobile Safety: An Analysis of Market Failure. *Bell Journal of Economcs*, Spring 1981, *12*, 27−48.

Ausness, Richard. High-Level Waste Management: The Nuclear Dilemma. *Wisconsin Law Review*, Fall 1979, *24(3)*, 98−113.

Baram, Michael S. *Alternatives to Regulation: Managing Risks to Health, Safety, and the Environment.* Lexington, MS.: Lexington Books 1982.

Bazelon, David. Risk and Responsibility. *Science,* July 1979, *205,* 277-280.

Bereano, Phillip L. Courts as Institutions for Assessing Technology. In W. A. Thomas (Ed.), *Scientists in the Legal System,* Ann Arbor: Ann Arbor Science Publishers, 1974.

Bingham, Gail. Does Negotiation Hold a Promise for Regulatory Reform? *Resolve,* Fall 1981, *Fall,* 1,3−6.

Blomquist, Glenn and Sam Peltzman. Passive Restraints: An Economist's View. In Robert W. Crandall and Lester B. Lave (Eds.), *The Scientific Basis of Health and Safety Regulation,* Washington, D.C.: Brookings Institution, 1981.

Bodansky, David and Fred H. Schmidt. Safety Aspects of Nuclear Energy. In Arthur W. Murphy (Ed.), *The Nuclear Power Controversy,* Englewood Cliffs, N.J.: Prentice-Hall, 1976.

Bogen, Kenneth T. Public Policy and Technological Risk. *IDEA: The Journal of Law and Technology,* 1980, *21,* 37−74.

Bogen, Kenneth T. Coordination of Regulatory Risk Analysis: Current Framework and Legislative Proposals. Congressional Research Service. Washington, D.C., June 19, 1981.

Brown, B. V. Projected Environmental Harm: Judicial Acceptance of a Concept of Uncertain Risk. *Journal of Urban Law,* 1976, *53,* 497−531.

Calabresi, Guido. *The Cost of Accidents: A Legal and Economic Analysis.* New Haven, CT: Yale University Press 1977.

Calkins, David R. et al. Identification, Characterization, and Control of Potential Human Carcinogens: A Framework for Federal Decision-Making. *Journal of the National Cancer Institute,* January 1980, *64,* 169−176.

Carnes, S.A., E. Copenhaver, J.H. Sorensen, E.J. Soderstrom, J.H. Reed, D.J. Bjornstadt, and E. Peelle. Incentives and Nuclear Waste Siting: Prospects and Constraints. In *Energy Systems and Policy,*: In press, 1984.

Casper, Barry M. Technology Policy and Democracy. *Science,* 1976, *194,* 29−35.

Clark, William C. Witches, Floods, and Wonder Drugs: Historical Perspectives on Risk Management. In Schwing and Albers, 1980.

Coates, Joseph F. Why Government Must Make A Mess of Technological Risk Management. In Hohenemser and Kasperson, 1982.

Cobb, Roger W. and Charles D. Elder. *Participation in American Politics: The Dynamics of Agenda-Building.* Boston: Allyn and Bacon 1972.

Cohen, Linda. *A Public Policy Approach to the Study of Optimal Compensation Systems: The Case of the Price-Anderson Act.* Discussion Paper 61-D, John F.Kennedy School of Goverment, Harvard University, February 1979.

Covello, Vincent T. and Joshua Menkes. Issues in Risk Analysis. In Hohenemser and Kasperson, 1982.

Crowfoot, James E. Negotiations: An Effective Tool for Citizen Organizations? *The NRAG Papers,* Fall 1980. *3,* 24−44.

Cyert, Richard and James March. *A Behavioral Theory of the Firm.* Englewood Cliffs, N.J.: Prentice-Hall 1963.

DeFinetti, Bruno, The True Subjectve Probability Problem. In C.A.S. Stael von Holstein (Ed.), *The Concept of Probability in Psychological Experiments,* Dordrecht, Holland: Reidel, 1974.

Dodge, Christopher H. and Robert L. Civiak. *Risk Assessment and Regulatory Policy.* Washington, D.C.: Congressional Research Service 1981.

Doniger, David D. *The Law and Policy of Toxic Substances Control.* Baltimore: John Hopkins University Press 1978.

Douglas, Mary and Aaron Wildavsky. *Risk and Culture.* Berkeley, CA.: University of California Press 1982.

Dowie, Mark et al. The Illusion of Safety, Part I. *Mother Jones,* June 1982, *VII,* 36−49.

Drechsler, T. Public Health Endangerment and Standards of Proof: Ethyl Corp. v. EPA. *Environmental Affairs*, 1977, *6*, 227−247.

Dyer, James S. An Asbestos Hazard Index for Managing Friable Asbestos Insulating Material. *Policy Sudies Review*, 1982, *1(4)*, 656−675.

Elandt-Johnson, Regina and Norman Johnson. *Survival Models and Data Analysis*. New York: Wiley Interscience 1980.

Field, Robert I. Statutory Language and Risk Management. Prepared for the Committee on Risk and Decision-Making, National Research Council 1981.

Fischhoff, Baruch. Cost-Benefit Analysis and the Art of Motorcycle Maintenance. *Policy Sciences*, 1977, *8*, 177-202.

Galanter, Marc. Why the 'Haves' Come Out Ahead. *Law and Society Review*, 1974, *9*, 95−160.

Goldsmith, R. I., and W. C. Banks. Environmental Values: Institutional Responsibility and the Supreme Court. *Harvard Environmental Law Review*, 1983, *7*, 1−40.

Gorinson, Stanley M. Three Mile Island: Lessons for the Government. In Hohenemser and Kasperson, 1982.

Graham, John D., Max Henrion and M. Granger Morgan. *An Analysis of Federal Policy Toward Automobile Safety Belts and Air Bags*. Working Paper, Carnegie-Mellon University, School of Urban and Public Affairs, Pittsburgh, PA, November 1981.

Graham, John D. Some Explanations for Disparities in Lifesaving Investments. *Policy Studies Review*, 1982, *1(4)*, 692−704.

Graham, John D. and Patricia Gorham. NHTSA and Passive Restraints: A Case of Arbitrary and Capricious Deregulation. *Administrative Law Review*, Spring 1983, *35*, 193−252.

Green, Harold P. and Alan Rosenthal. *Government of the Atom: The Integration of Powers*. New York: Atherton 1963.

Green, Harold P. "The Role of Law in Determining Acceptability of Risk. In Schwing and Albers, 1980.

Gross, Jonathan L. and Steve Rayner. *Measuring Culture: A Paradigm for the Analysis of Social Organization*. New York: Columbia University Press, in press 1983.

Grumbly, Thomas. The Political Culture and Management Opportunities of Regulatory Science. Testimony before the Committee on Institutional Means for Assessment of Risks to Public Health, National Research Council. Washington, D.C., February 10, 1982.

Gusman, Sam. Policy Dialogue. *Environmental Comment*, 1981, *November*, 14−16.

Hadden, Susan G. Technical Information for Citizen Participation. *Journal of Applied Behavioral Science*, 1981, *17(4)*, 537−549.

Harris, Louis and Associates. *Risk in a complex society: A Marsh and McLennan Public Opinion Survey*. New York: Marsh and McLennan 1980.

Hart Associates, Inc. *Public Attitudes Toward Passive Restraint Systems*. Washington, D.C.: U.S. Department of Transportation, NHTSA 1978. DOT-HS-803-567.

Harter, Philip J. *Negotiating Regulations: A Cure for the Malaise?* Technical Report, Administrative Conference of the United States, 1982. Washington, D.C.

Hohenemser, Christoph, and Jeanne X. Kasperson, Eds. *Risk in a Technological Society*. Boulder, Colorado: Westview Press 1982.

Howard, Ronald A. On Making Life and Death Decisions. In Schwing and Albers, 1980.

Huntington, Samuel P. Congressional Responses to the Twentieth Century. In David B. Truman (Ed.), *The Congress and America's Future*, 2nd ed., Englewood Cliffs, N.J.: Prentice-Hall, 1973.

Interagency Regulatory Liaison Group (IRLG). *Scientific Basis for Identifying Potential Carcinogens and Estimating Their Risks*. Washington, D.C.: Work Group on Risk Assessment February, 1979.

Kahneman, Daniel, Paul Slovic and Amos Tversky, Eds. *Judgment under uncertainty: Heuristics and biases*. Cambridge: Cambridge University Press 1982.

Kantrowitz, Arthur. Proposal for an Institution for Scientific Judgment. *Science*, May 1976, *156*, 763−764.

Kasperson, Roger E. Societal Management of Technological Hazards. In Robert W. Kates (Ed.), *Managing Technological Hazard: Research Needs and Opportunities,* Boulder, Colo.: University of Colorado Institute of Behavioral Science, 1977.

Kates, Robert W. Summary Report. In Robert W. Kates (Ed.), *Managing Technological Hazard: Research Needs and Opportunities,* Boulder, Colo.: University of Colorado Institute of Behavioral Science, 1977.

Kendall, Henry W., Study Director. *The Risks of Nuclear Power Reactors: A Review of the NRC Reactor Safety Study.* Cambridge, Mass.: Union of Concerned Scientists 1977.

Kendall, Henry W., Study Director. *The Risks of Nuclear Power Reactors: A Review of the NRC Reactor Safety Study.* Cambridge, Mass.: Union of Concerned Scientists 1977.

Kevin, D. *Federal/State Relations in Radioactive Waste Management Oceans Program.* Washington, D.C.: U.S. Congress, Office of Technology Assessment 1980.

Knight, Frank. *Risk, Uncertainty, and Profit.* Chicago: University of Chicago Press 1971 (1921).

Kraft, Michael E. *Risk Analysis in the Legislative Process: Congress and Risk Management Decisionmaking.* Redondo Beach, California: J.H. Wiggins Company June, 1982. Technical Report No. 82-1398-2.

Kraft, Michael E. *The Use of Risk Analysis in Federal Regulatory Agencies: Problems and Prospects.* Redondo Beach, California: J.H. Wiggins Company June, 1982. Technical Report No. 82-1398-3.

Kunreuther, Howard. Limited Knowledge and Insurance Protection. *Public Policy,* Spring 1976, *24(2),* 227–261.

Kunreuther, Howard, et al. *Disaster Insurance Protection: Public Policy Lessons.* New York: Wiley 1978.

Lake, Laura M. *Environmental Mediation: The Search for Consensus.* Boulder, Colo.: Westview Press 1980.

Landau, Martin. Redundancy, Rationality, and the Problem of Duplication and Overlap, *Public Administration Review,* July/August 1969, *29,* 346–358.

LaPorte, Todd. Nuclear Waste: Increasing Scale and Sociopolitical Impact. *Science,* 1978, *207,* 22.

Latin, Howard A. The Significance of Toxic Health Risks: An Essay on Legal Decision-making Under Uncertainty. *Ecology Law Quarterly,* 1982, *10,* 339–396.

Lave, Lester B. *Quantitative Risk Assessment in Regulation.* Washington, D.C.: Brookings Institution 1983.

Lawless, E. W. *Technology and Social Shock.* Kansas City: Midwest Research Institute 1974.

Lee, Kai N. A Federalist Strategy for Nuclear Waste Management. *Science,* 1980, *208,* 679.

Leventhal, H. Environmental Decisionmaking and the Role of the Courts. *University of Pennsylvania Law Review,* 1974, *122,* 509–555.

Lilley, William and James C. Miller III. The New 'Social Regulation'. *Public Interest,* Spring 1977, *47,* 49–61.

Lindblom, Charles E. The Science of Muddling Through. *Public Administration Review,* Spring 1959, *19,* 79–88.

Linneroth, J. *Evaluation of life saving: A survey.* Research Report RR 75–21, IIASA, 1975.

Lovins, A. Cost-Benefit Assessments in Energy Policy. *George Washington Law Review,* 1977, *45,* 911.

Lowrance, William. *Of acceptable risk: Science and the determination of safety.* Los Altos, California: William Kaufman 1976.

Lowrance, William. The Nature of Risk. In Schwing and Albers, 1980.

Lund, Adrian and Allan F. Williams. *Public Opinion Surveys on Automatic Crash Protection.* Research Note Number 102, Institue for Highway Safety, Washington, D.C., 1982.

Lundstrom, Louis C. Integrating Vehicle Safety, Cost and Consumer Attitudes. In *The Fourth International Congress on Automotive Safety,* Washington, D.C.: U.S. Department of Transportation, NHTSA, July, 1975.

MacLean, D. *Risk and Consent: A Survey of Issues for Centralized Decision Making.* College Park, MD.: University of Maryland, Center for Philosophy and Public Policy 1980.

Markey, Harold T. Science and Law: A Dialogue on Understanding. *American Bar Association Journal,* 1982, *68,* 154–158.

Mars, G. *Cheats at Work: An Anthropology of Workplace Crime.* London: George Allen and Unwin 1982.

Matheny, Albert R. and Bruce A. Williams. Scientific Disputes and Adversary Procedures in Policy-Making: An Evaluation of the Science Court. *Law & Policy Quarterly,* July 1981, *2,* 341–364.

Matheny, Albert R. and Bruce A. Williams. Regulation, Risk Assessment, and the Supreme Court: The Case of OSHA's Cancer Policy. Unpublished manuscript, 1983.

Mazur, Allan. Disputes Between Experts. *Minerva,* April 1973, *XI,* 243–262.

Mendeloff, John. *Regulating Safety: An Economic and Political Analysis of Occupational Safety and Health Policy.* Cambridge, Massachusetts: MIT Press 1979.

Melnick, R. S. Judicial Capacity and Environmental Litigation: The Case of the Clean Air Act. Paper presented to the Annual Meeting of the American Political Science Association, Washington, D.C., 1980.

Moss, Thomas H. Environmental versus emission control costs—a legislative perspective. In D. S. Shriner, C. R. Richmond, and S. E. Lindberg (Eds.), *Atmospheric sulfur deposition: Environmental impact and health effects,* Ann Arbor: Ann Arbor Science Publishers, 1980.

Moss, Thomas and Barry Lubin. Risk Analysis: A Legislative Perspective. In Richmond, Walsh, and Copenhauer, 1981, q.v.

Nader, Ralph and John Abbotts. *The Menace of Atomic Energy.* New York: W. W. Norton and Co. 1979.

National Academy of Sciences, Committee on Nuclear and Alternative Energy Systems. *Energy In Transition: 1985-2010.* San Francisco: W. H. Freeman 1979.

National Research Council, Committee on Risk and Decision Making. *Risk and Decision Making: Perspectives and Research.* Washington, D.C.: National Academy Press 1982.

National Research Council. *Background Materials for Committee on the Institutional Means for Assessment of Risks to Public Health.* Washington, D.C.: National Research Council 1982.

National Research Council, Commission on Life Sciences, Committee on the Institutional Means for Assessment of Risks to Public Health. *Risk Assessment in the Federal Government: Managing the Process.* Washington, D. C.: National Research Council 1983.

Nelkin, Dorothy and Michael Pollack, Problems and procedures in the regulation of technological risk. In Carol H. Weiss and Allen H. Barton (Eds.), *Making Bureaucracies Work,* Beverly Hills, Calif.: Sage Publications, 1980.

Nelkin, Dorothy. Some Social and Political Dimensions of Nuclear Power: Examples From Three Mile Island. *American Political Science Review,* March 1981, *75(1),* 132–142.

Nemetz, Peter N. and Adrian R. Vining. The Biology-Pathology Interface: Theories of Pathogenesis, Benefit Valuation and Public Policy Formation. *Policy Sciences,* 1981, *13,* 125–138.

Nyhart, J. D. *Science, Technology and Judicial Decision-Making: An Exploratory Discussion.* Washington D. C.: National Science Foundation 1981. Proceedings of Conference sponsored by the Massachusetts Institute of Technology and the National Science Foundation, September, 1977.

Oakes, J. L. The Judicial Role in Environmental Law. *New York University Law Review,* 1977, *52,* 498–517.

O'Brien, David M. The Courts, Technology Assessment, and Science-Policy Disputes. In David M. O'Brien and D. A. Marchand (Eds.), *The Politics of Technology Assessment,* Lexington, Mass.: Lexington Books, 1982.

O'Connor, W. A. Incentives for the Construction of Low-Level Nuclear Waste Facilities. In *Low-Level Waste: A Program for Action*, Washington, D.C.: Report of the National Governors' Association Task Force on Low-Level Radioactive Waste Disposal, 1980.

Ogul, Morris S. *Congress oversees the bureaucracy: Studies in legislative supervision.* Pittsburgh: University of Pittsburgh Press 1976.

O'Hare, Michael. Not on My Block You Don't: Facility Siting and the Strategic Importance of Compensation. *Public Policy,* 1977, *25(407),* 407.

Olsen, Mancur. *The Logic of Collective Action: Public Goods and the Theory of Groups.* Cambridge, MA.: Harvard University Press 1965.

O'Neill, Brian, Allan F. William, and Ronald S. Karpf. Passenger Car Size and Driver Seat Belt Use. *American Journal of Public Health,* 1983.

Opinion Research Corporation (ORC). *Safety Belt Usage Among Drivers.* Washington, D.C.: U.S. Department of Transportation, NHTSA 1980. DOT-HS-805-227.

Peterson, Rusell W. Three Mile Island: Lessons for America. In Honenemser and Kasperson, 1982, q.v.

Pringle, P. and J. Spigelman. *The Nuclear Barons.* New York: Holt-Rinehart and Winston 1981.

Rayner, Steve. The Perception of Time and Space in Egalitarian Sects: A Millenarian Cosmology. In M. Douglas (Ed.), *Essays in the Sociology of Perception,* London: Routledge and Kegan Paul, 1982.

Regens, James L., Thomas M. Dietz, and Robert W. Rycroft. Risk Assessment in the Policy-Making Process: Environmental Health and Safety Protection. *Public Administration Review,* March/April 1983, *43,* 166−175.

Ricci, Leda. *National Crash Severity Study Statistics.* Washington, D.C.: U.S. Department of Transportation, NHTSA 1979, DOT-HS-805-227.

Ricci, Paolo F. and Lawrence S. Molton. Risk and Benefit in Environmental Law. *Science,* December 1981, *214(4525),* 1096−1100.

Richmond, Chester R., Phillip J. Walsh and Emily D. Copenhauer. *Health Risk Analysis: Proceedings of the Third Life Sciences Symposium.* Philadelphia, PA.: Franklin Institute Press 1981.

Robertson, Leon S. Car Crashes: Perceived Vulnerability and Willingness to Pay for Crash Protection. *Journal of Community Health,* Winter 1977, *3,* 136−141.

Rodgers, William H. A Hard Look at Vermont Yankee: Environmental Law Under Close Scrutiny. *Georgetown Law Journal,* 1979, *67,* 699-727.

Rogovin, Mitchell. *Three Mile Island: A Report to the Commission and to the Public.* Technical Report Vol. 1, Nuclear Regulatory Commission, 1980.

Rowe, W.C. *An Anatomy of Risk.* New York: John Wiley 1977.

Rushefsky, Mark. Technical Disputes: Why Experts Disagree. *Policy Studies Review,* May 1982, *1,* 676−685.

Rushefsky, Mark. The Misuse of Science in Governmental Decision Making. In progress.

Sabatier, Paul. Regulatory policy-making: Toward a framework of analysis. *Natural Resources Journal,* July 1977, *17,* 415−460.

Salisbury, Robert H. Why No Corporatism in America? In Phillipe C. Schmitter and Gerhard Lehmbruch (Eds.), *Trends Toward Corporatist Intermediation,* Beverly Hills, CA.: Sage Publications, 1979.

Salsburg, David and Andrew Heath. When Science Progresses and Bureaucracies Lag—The Case of Cancer Research. *The Public Interest,* Fall 1981, *65,* 30−39.

Sandler, Ross. Law: EPA's Secret "Science Courts". *Environment,* January/February 1982, *24,* 4−5.

Scalia, Antonin. Vermont Yankee: The APA, the D. C. Circuit, and the Supreme Court. In Philip B. Kurland and G. Casper (Eds.), *The Supreme Court Review, 1978,* Chicago: University of Chicago Press, 1979.

Scalia, Antonin. A Note on the Benzene Case. *Regulation: AEI Journal on Government and Society,* 1980, *July/August,* 25−28.

Schmandt, Jurgen. Toward a Theory of the Modern State: Administrative versus Scientific State. In Joseph S. Szyliowicz (Ed.), *Technology and International Affairs,* New York: Preager, 1981.

Schmandt, Jurgen. Regulatory Reform as a Management Task: Linking Analysis to Decision Making. Paper prepared for the 1982 annual meeting of the Association for Public Policy and Management. October, 1982.

Schuck, Peter H. Litigaton, Bargaining, and Regulation. *Regulation,* July/August 1979, *3,* 26–34.

Schurr, Sam H. et al. *Energy in America's Future.* Baltimore, MD.: Johns Hopkins University Press 1979.

Schwalm, Norman D. and Paul Slovic. *Development and Test of a Motivational Approach and Materials for Increasing Use of Restraints.* Washington, D.C.: U.S. Department of Transportation, NHTSA 1982.

Schwing, Richard C. and Walter A. Albers, Jr., Eds. *Societal Risk Assessment: How Safe Is Safe Enough?* New York: Plenum Press 1980.

Selznick, Philip. *TVA and the Grass Roots.* (Berkeley: University of California Press, 1949.

Shapiro, Martin. Judicial Activism. In S. M. Lipset (Ed.), *The Third Century,* Stanford, CA.: Hoover Institution Press, 1979.

Sherman, Roger. *The Economics of Industry.* Boston: Little, Brown 1974.

Sills, David L. A Comment on Dorothy Nelkin's 'Some Social and Political Dimensions of Nuclear Power: Examples from Three Mile Island'. *American Political Science Review,* March 1981, *75(1),* 143–145.

Slovic, Paul, Baruch Fischhoff, and Sarah Lichtenstein. Accident Probabilities and Seat Belt Usage: A Psychological Perspective. *Accident Analysis and Prevention,* 1978, *10,* 281–285.

Slovic, Paul, Baruch Fischhoff, and Sarah Lichtenstein. Facts and Fears: Understanding Perceived Risk. In Schwing and Albers, 1980.

Solomon, Kenneth Alvin, and David Okrent. Some Comments on De Facto Limits on Liability. Rand Corp. P-5885, June 1977.

Starr, Chauncey. Societal benefit versus technological risk. *Science,* September 1969, *165,* 1232–1238.

Stewart, Richard B. The Reformation of American Administrative Law. *Harvard Law Review,* 1975, *88,* 1667–1813.

Stewart, Richard B. Judging the Imponderables of Environmental Policy: Judicial Review Under the Clean Air Act. In A. F. Friedlaender (Ed.), *Approaches to Controlling Air Pollution,* Cambridge, Mass.: MIT Press, 1978.

Susskind, Lawrence and Alan Weinstein. Towards a Theory of Environmental Dispute Resolution. *Boston College Environmental Affairs Law Review,* June 1980, *9,* 311–357.

Swartzman, Daniel, Richard A. Liroff, and Kevin G. Croke, Eds. *Cost-benefit analysis and environmental regulation: Politics, ethics, and methods.* Washington, D.C.: Conservation Foundation 1982.

Task Force of the Presidential Advisory Group on Anticipated Advances in Science and Technology. The Science Court Experiment: An Interim Report. *Science,* August 1976, *193,* 652–656.

Teknekron Research, Inc. *1979 Survey of Public Perceptions of Highway Safety.* Washington, D.C.: U.S. Department of Transportation, NHTSA 1979.

Thaler, Richard and Sherwin Rosen. The Value of Saving a Life: Evidence from the Labor Market. In N. Terleckyj (Ed.), *Household Production and Consumption,* New York: Columbia University Press, 1975.

Thompson, Michael. *Beyond Self-Interest: A Cultural Analysis of a Risk Debate.* Working Paper, International Institute for Applied Systems Analysis, 1981. Laxenburg, Austria.

Thompson, Michael. *Among the Energy Tribes: The Anthropology of the Current Policy Debate.* Working Paper, International Institute for Applied Systems Analysis, 1982.

Tobin, Richard J. *The Social Gamble: Determining Acceptable Levels of Air Quality.* Lexington, MA.: D.C. Health and Company 1979.

U.S. Congress, House of Representatives. Subcommittee on Science, Research and Technology of the Committee on Science and Technology. *Comparative Risk Assessment: Hearings Before the Subcommittee.* Washington, D.C.: Government Printing Office 1980. 96th Congress, 2nd Session.

U.S. Congress. Joint Hearings. *Risk/Benefit Analysis in the Legislative Process.* Washington, D.C.: Government Printing Office 1980. Joint hearings before the Subcommittee on Science, Research, and Technology of the Committee on Science and Technology, U.S. House of Representatives, and the Subcommittee on Science, Technology, and Space of the Committee on Commerce, Science, and Transportation, United States Senate and Congress/Science Forum with the American Association for the Advancement of Science, 96th Congress, 1st Session.

U.S. Congress, Office of Technology Assessment, *Technology Assessment Activities in the Industrial, Academic, and Governmental Communities.* Washington, D.C.: U.S. Government Printing Office 1976.

U.S. Congress, Office of Technology Assessment. *Direct Use of Coal.* Washington, D.C.: U.S. Government Printing Office 1978.

U.S. Congress Office of Technology Assessment. *Assessment of Technologies for Determining Cancer Risks in the Environment.* Washington, D.C.: Government Printing Office 1981.

U.S. Congress, Senate, Select Committee on Small Business and Subcommittee on Oversight of Government Management of the Committee on Governmental Affairs. *Hearings on Regulatory Negotiations.* Washington D.C.: Government Printing Office 1980. 96th Congress, 2nd Session; July 29 and 30.

U.S. Environmental Protection Agency, Office of Research and Development. *Air Quality Criteria for Lead.* Washington, D.C.: U.S. Government Printing Office 1977.

U.S. Environmental Protection Agency. *Background Support Document for Economic Impact Assessment of the Lead Ambient Air Quality Standard.* Washington, D.C.: U.S. Government Printing Office 1978.

U.S. Environmental Protection Agency, Office of Water and Waste Management. Siting of Hazardous Waste Management Facilities and Public Opposition. Prepared by Centaur Associates for EPA, Washington, D.C., 1979.

U.S. Environmental Protection Agency. *Comparisons of Estimated and Actual Pollution Control Costs for Selected Industries.* Washington, D.C.: Government Printing Office 1980.

Vig, Norman J. Environmental Decision Making in the Lower Courts: the Reserve Mining Case. In M. Steinman (Ed.), *Energy and Environmental Issues,* Lexington, Mass.: Lexington Books, 1979.

Villmoare, Adelaide H. State and Legal Authority: A Context for the Analysis of Judicial Policy-Making. *Law & Policy Quarterly,* January 1982, *4,* 5–36.

Viscusi, W. Kip. *Risk by Choice: Regulating Health and Safety in the Workplace.* Cambridge, MA.: Harvard University Press 1983.

Viscusi, W. Kip. *Regulating Product Safety.* Washington, D.C.: American Enterprise Institute forthcoming.

Warren, Jacqueline M. and Ross Sandler. Law: EPA's Failure to Regulate Toxic Chemicals. *Environment,* December 1981, *23,* 2–4.

Weber, Max. *The Theory of Social and Economic Organization.* New York: The Free Press 1947.

Weinberg, Alvin M. Science and Trans-Science. *Minerva,* April 1972, *X,* 209–222.

Weisberger, John H. and Gary M. Williams. Carcinogen Testing: Current Problems and New Approaches. *Science,* 23 October, 1981, *214,* 401–407.

Wenner, Lottie, M. *The Environmental Decade in Court.* Bloomington: Indiana University Press 1982.

Whitehead, Alfred North. *Science and the Modern World.* New York: The Free Press 1926.

Wildavsky, Aaron. No risk is the highest risk of all. *American Scientist*, January-February 1979, *67*, 32−37.

Wilson, Richard. Analyzing the daily risks of life. *Technology Review*, 1979, *18*, 39−45.

Wilson, James Q., Ed. *The Politics of Regulation*. New York: Basic Books 1980.

Wolf, Charles, Jr. A Theory of Non-Market Failures. *The Public Interest*, Spring 1979, *55*, 114−133.

Wood, William C. *Insuring Nuclear Power: Liability, Safety, and Ecnomic Efficiency*. Greenwich, CN.: JAI Press, Inc. 1982.

Wood, William C. Putting a Price on Radiation. *Journal of Policy Analysis and Management*, Winter 1983, *2(2)*, 291−295.

Wynne, Brian. Rationality and Ritual: The Windscale Inquiry and Nuclear Decisions in Britain. British Society for the History of Science, Monograph 3. Chalfont St. Giles, 1982.

Zeckhauser, Richard and David Shepard. Where now for saving lives? *Law and Contemporary Problems*, 1976, *40(4)*, 5−45.

Zimmerman, Rae T. Formation of New Organizations to Manage Risk. *Policy Studies Review*, 1982, *1(4)*, 736−48.

INDEX